An
Introduction to Child Study

"Take heed that ye despise not one of these little ones."—Matthew 18:10.

An
INTRODUCTION
to
CHILD STUDY

By

CLARENCE H. BENSON

*Director of the Christian Education Course of the
Moody Bible Institute of Chicago
Secretary of the Evangelical Teacher Training Association
Editor of the All Bible Graded Lesson Series*

*Author of
Brief Bible Outline; The Sunday School in Action;
The Earth the Theater of the Universe; The Church
at Work; A Guide for Bible Study; Intermediate
Curriculum for the Standard Vacation Bible Course*

CHICAGO
THE BIBLE INSTITUTE COLPORTAGE ASS'N
843-845 NORTH WELLS STREET

Printed in the United States of America

AFFECTIONATELY
DEDICATED TO MY TWO
BOYS, CHARLES FRANCIS AND
CLARK DAVID, WHO HAVE BEEN
A GREAT SOURCE OF INSPIRATION
AND INSTRUCTION IN THE
STUDY OF CHILDHOOD
AND ADOLESCENCE

PREFACE

IN RECENT years when the revival of religious education has created a new interest in child study, many books have been written, and the question might well be raised as to what a new author might add to the present library of publications. But while the field of psychology is vast and the writers numerous, only a comparative few are free from serious criticism. The average psychologist rejects the sound, sane teachings of earlier days and refuses to accept the child upon the basis so clearly taught in the Bible. The strange, wild theories that are advanced seem to originate from the vain imaginations of what children like to be or what they ought to be rather than what they actually are. Child nature is no different today from what it was a thousand years ago. The Bible along with history and our every-day experience teaches us that in spite of all we can do in an educational way the child will go in the wrong direction. The failure of modern education to recognize this fact is the cause of its failure to meet the needs of the present-day world. Before education can perform its proper task among men it must recognize that this task is not to lift a rising race but a falling one. The natural inclination of the child is downward. Modern enlightenment cannot alter this scriptural teaching. The only factor in our civilization that was not among the nations that are gone is the Bible, and a psychology that is not founded upon its tenets can never produce an abiding race.

The results of a widespread propaganda of this materialistic and mechanical psychology are already apparent in our nation. An intellectual shallowness which ignores the attitude of average men and women to the simplest questions of right and wrong is sure to prove disastrous. There never was a period in American history when there was less religion taught in the home and in the school than today, and there is no civilized nation that approximates our deplorable record of divorces and juvenile crime. The problems of our church, the failures of our schools, in fact, the ills of our nation, can be traced largely to our homes where fathers and mothers, lacking in spiritual depth of character and unfit to be the teachers of the children, are assuming the grave responsibility of rearing and educating our future nation. Today we have 27,000,000 boys and girls classified as Protestants who are growing up practically without any religious education. In a few decades they will constitute the forces that will mold and make the masses of America.

The impending disaster that must sooner or later overtake the nation can be averted only by the right training of childhood and youth. "A despotism can prosper," says Irving Bacheller, "as did pagan Rome by main strength without the careful training of the young. A democracy is different. Its young are to be its rulers and therefore must be trained." The founders of America believed that the Bible should be taught in home, school and church and the younger generation made amenable to its discipline. "Without this discipline," says Bacheller, "they seemed to understand that a democracy must fail. 'Look after the boys and girls,' they said, 'and your men and women can be trusted. Let them first learn to obey and then put the fear and love of God in them.' If this is done for all, each will live in security and faith in his fellow-men and in his government.''

Child study, then, instead of being shunned because of its materialistic associations, should receive more attention than ever from parents and teachers. There is a safe and sound psychology with which all responsible for the building of the nation should be familiar. Such a work the author has attempted to provide. It is not a psychology in the strictest sense of the term, for it deals with other aspects of child life besides the mental characteristics. Moreover no attempt has been made to furnish an exhaustive treatise for the advanced student. It is simply intended as an introduction to the subject in connection with the entire program of religious education and is naturally a book for beginners.

The author is indebted to the contributions of many writers whom he has quoted freely and frequently in compiling this work. Mention of their names in most instances has accompanied such references, and in addition a bibliography of the books which have been consulted has been appended. This however does not mean that all the statements of these writers are endorsed, as some have been consulted for their suggestions regarding teaching methods rather than their erroneous conceptions of teaching material.

C. H. B.

Since the publication of the former editions, the model Sunday-school curriculum for grade and high school pupils set forth in these pages, has been completed by the classes in Curriculum Making of the Moody Bible Institute, and is now published by the Scripture Press under the caption the All Bible Graded Series. Further projects of this class will include a supplemental Vacation Bible School course, and a program for the Week Day Church School and Christian Endeavor Societies, which will be correlated with the All Bible Graded Series for the Sunday-school. This will provide the long-sought comprehensive, consecutive, correlated, and complete instruction for the tri-weekly Church School.

C. H. B.

CONTENTS

CHAP.   PAGE

PREFACE - - - - - - - - - - - - - - 7

I   THE IMPORTANCE OF LIFE - - - - - - - - 19

1. Value.
    a. Human estimates.
    b. God's estimate.
    c. Christ's estimate.

2. Extent.

3. Possibilities.
    a. Knowledge.
    b. Freedom.
    c. Possession.
    d. Power.
    e. Happiness.

II   THE IMPORTANCE OF CHILD LIFE - - - - - - 25

1. Christ was a child.

2. Christ magnified child life.
    a. He put the child and not the adult in the center of the group.
    b. He rebuked the disciples when they argued that adults had prior claim to His time.
    c. He emphasized the place and importance of child training in the church.

3. The child life ministers to mankind.
    a. Builders of the home.
    b. Builders of society.
    c. Religious leaders of mankind.

4. The child life is plastic.

III   THE IMPORTANCE OF CHILD STUDY - - - - - 32

The definition of Child Study suggests

1. Knowledge of a person.
    a. Know God.
    b. Know man.
        (1) Know children.

2. Knowledge of a law.
    a. Life can be planned.
    b. Tragedies may be prevented.
    c. Our hope is formation and regeneration rather than reformation.
        (1) Life's mistakes cannot be wholly rectified.
        (2) Our business is to bring a cargo and not a derelict into port.
        (3) Life's success depends upon obedience to God's laws.

3. Knowledge of development or growth.
    The work of the teacher.
    a. Not molding plastic clay.
    b. Not preserving from evil.
    c. Not teaching little men.
    d. But building a life.
        (1) Determining a Christian.
        (2) Developing a personality.
            (a) In the material world.
            (b) In the religious world.

IV SOURCES OF CHILD STUDY - - - - - - - - 43

1. Observation.
2. Reminiscence.
3. Literature.
4. Science.

V THREE FORCES IN LIFE BUILDING - - - - - 47

1. Heredity.
    a. Children inherit tendencies, not character.
    b. Heredity is determined by grandparents rather than parents.
    c. Heredity is more marked in adolescence than in childhood.

2. Environment.
    a. The home.
        (1) The mother.
        (2) The father.
    b. The community.

   (1) The school.
   (2) The church.
   (3) The gang.
  3. Personality.
   a. Habits shape a personality.
   b. Expression intensifies a personality.
   c. Religion controls a personality.

VI THREE PHASES OF RELIGIOUS EDUCATION - - 63

  1. Information.

  2. Worship.
   a. Attendance.
   b. Punctuality.
   c. Offering.

  3. Expression.

  4. The threefold program of training.
   a. The modified Sunday-school.
   b. The tri-weekly church school.

VII THREE FIELDS OF RELIGIOUS EDUCATION - - 74

  1. The home.
   a. The Jewish home.
   b. The colonial home.
   c. The modern home.

  2. The school.
   a. The Jewish school.
   b. The parochial school.
   c. The public school.

  3. The church.
   a. Churches are built and equipped for adults rather than children.
   b. Church programs are primarily prepared for adults.
   c. Ministers are trained to preach rather than to teach.
   d. The Sunday-school is inadequately financed.
   e. The Sunday-school is inadequately organized and graded.

VIII   Periods of Child Study - - - - - - - 87

1. Infancy, 0-3.
2. Early Childhood, 4-5.
3. Middle Childhood, 6-8.
4. Later Childhood, 9-11.
5. Early Adolescence, 12-14.
6. Middle Adolescence, 15-17.
7. Later Adolescence, 18-24.

IX   Infancy - - - - - - - - - - - - - - 91

1. Physically he is an *actor*.
    a. Activity is essential to growth.
    b. Activity is essential to development.
    c. Generated energy requires an outlet.
    d. The nervous system requires a response to impressions.
        (1) Instincts impel actions.
        (2) Ideas impel actions.

2. Mentally he is a *discoverer*.
    a. He discovers his mother.
    b. He discovers his world.
    c. He discovers himself.

3. Religiously he is an *imitator*.
    a. His religion will be a reflection of the religion he finds about him.
    b. His moral habits and attitudes will be largely determined by others.
    c. Adult approval or disapproval of his first acts will be far-reaching.

4. Training.
    a. The Cradle Roll.
        (1) To enroll a new scholar for the Sunday-school.
        (2) To establish a point of contact between church and home.
        (3) To enlist parental training.
    b. Cradle Roll class.

X   Early Childhood - - - - - - - - - - 105

1. Physically he is a *player*.
    a. Play is a physical trainer.

    b. Play is a mental instructor.
        (1) Childish instincts expressed in play.
        (2) Childish imaginations expressed in play.
        (3) Childish imitations expressed in play.
    c. Play is a social equalizer.
    d. Play is a moral teacher.

  2. Mentally he is a *questioner*.
    a. Inquisitiveness affects education.
    b. Inquisitiveness affects personality.

  3. Religiously he is a *believer*.
    a. Exaggerated statements.
    b. Inaccurate replies.
    c. Profitable deception.

  4. Training.
    a. Worship.
        (1) Praise.
        (2) Prayer.
        (3) Giving.
    b. Instruction.
        (1) God as a Heavenly Father.
        (2) Nature lessons.
        (3) Child lessons.
    c. Discipline.

XI MIDDLE CHILDHOOD - - - - - - - - - - 123

  1. Physically he is a *hustler*.
    a. Play.
        (1) He no longer plays alone.
        (2) His play is more purposeful.
        (3) Play and playmates will be determined by
               sex.
    b. Work.
        (1) Educative value.
        (2) Social value.
        (3) Moral value.

  2. Mentally he is an *observer*.
    a. The law of apperception.
    b. Physical efficiency.

3. Religiously he is a *discriminator*.
   a. Fact and fiction.
   b. Right and wrong.
   c. Precept and practice.

4. Training.
   a. Manual activity.
   b. Comprehensive worship.
   c. Reverence.
      (1) Order.
      (2) Regularity.

XII LATER CHILDHOOD - - - - - - - - - 147

1. Physically he is a *rover*.
   a. This is a period of health and hardihood.
   b. Love of nature.

2. Mentally he is an *investigator*.
   a. Collections.
   b. Mechanical interests.
   c. Reading.
   d. Memory.
      (1) Repetition.
      (2) Association.

3. Socially he is a *gangster*.
   a. Dislike of the opposite sex.
   b. Tendency for organization.

4. Spiritually he is a *worshiper*.

5. Training.
   a. The use of the Sabbath.
   b. The use of the Bible.
   c. Memory work.
   d. Experience and training in worship.
   e. Decision and church membership.
      (1) Twelve was an important age in Jewish life.
      (2) Many great and good men date their conversion from childhood.
      (3) Childhood is followed by a period of temporary religious decline.
      (4) The great majority of boys and girls drop out of the Sunday-school during the days of early adolescence.

(5) Child conversions are permanent conversions.

(6) Decisions for Christ in childhood prepare the way for other important decisions in adolescence.

XIII Early Adolescence - - - - - - - - 171

1. The principal physical characteristic is *change*.
   a. In body.
   b. In ideals.
   c. In pursuits.
   d. In disposition.

2. The principal mental characteristic is *criticism*.
   a. Adolescent education should include a wide variety of subjects.
   b. Adolescent education should deal with knowledge *en masse*.
   c. Intellectual capacities that are not started or stimulated in early adolescence may be lost.

3. The principal social characteristic is *companionship*.
   a. In the home.
   b. In school.
   c. In the gang.
   d. In church.

4. The principal spiritual characteristic is *conversion*.
   a. Conversions of early youth involve the personality.
   b. Conversions reach their peak in early youth.
   c. Conversion in early youth prevents incorrigibility.

5. Training.
   a. Organized departments.
   b. Organized classes.
   c. Graded lessons.
   d. Trained leadership.
      (1) Keep open the channels of communication.
      (2) Multiply the interests.
      (3) Command by counsel.
      (4) Control by companionship.

XIV Later Adolescence - - - - - - - - - 201

1. The principal physical characteristic is *achievement*.

2. The principal mental characteristic is *power*.
    a. Knowledge.
    b. Control.
    c. Independence.

3. The principal social characteristic is *friendship*.
    a. The breaking of home ties.
    b. Awakening of altruism and patriotism.
    c. Manifestation of mating and homing instincts.

4. The principal spiritual characteristic is *instability*.
    a. Certain hindrances.
        (1) Doubt.
        (2) Worldliness.
    b. Certain helps.
        (1) Deepening love of nature.
        (2) Increased vigor of will.

5. Training.
    a. Class organization.
        (1) Class rooms.
        (2) Self-government.
        (3) Social contacts.
        (4) Class activities.
    b. Appropriate curriculum.
    c. Vocational appeal.
        (1) Christian stewardship.
        (2) Christian heroes.
        (3) Christian ministry.

Bibliography - - - - - - - - - - - - - - 233

Appendix (Child Crime and Religious Instruction) 235

AN INTRODUCTION TO CHILD STUDY

I

THE IMPORTANCE OF LIFE

HENRY DRUMMOND tells us that the greatest thing in the world is love, but there is something in this world greater than love. Life is the greatest thing in the world. Christ in coming expressed the great love of God, but He came that men might have life. There is a vast difference between the making of a living and the making of a life. Truly "a man's life consisteth not in the abundance of things which he possesseth." The importance of life may be realized from three things.

1. Value.

What is the value of a life? Let us consider

a. Human estimate.

Estimates of the value of life vary in different parts of the earth. In some places life is held in small regard.

On the banks of the Congo river a life is worth but a tusk of ivory. In India and China infanticides are still common. The Japanese take revenge on their enemies by committing suicide on their doorstep. We boast that in our civilized country there is the highest estimate placed upon life. However, in this day we have forgotten its value. Last year in America there were 15,000 suicides and 10,000 homicides, many for trivial causes. The recklessness with which firearms are handled and automobiles are operated, leads one to believe that life is little esteemed. No human estimates can determine the immeasurable, incomprehensible value of life. Other sources must be investigated for an answer to this question.

b. God's estimate.

Genesis 9:6. Before the flood, crime went unpunished. Murderers were never condemned nor executed and the world was at its worst. After the deluge God committed the judicial functions into the hands of man with this stipulation—"Whoso sheddeth man's blood by man shall his blood be shed, for in the image of God made he man." Regardless of man's attitude toward capital punishment it is evident that God set forth at this particular time in the period of earth's history, His law of life. Regardless of justice or mercy there was only one way in which life could be valued. Life could not be balanced by stocks or bonds, lands or gold. Nothing but the equivalency of another life would suffice.

c. Christ's estimate.

Mark 8:36. "What shall it profit a man if he shall gain the whole world and lose his own soul?" No one ever gained the world. No one ever gained the greater part of the world. Earth's most eminent men have had to be content with a smaller conquest, but Christ said that if a man gained the whole world it could not be equivalent to his life. Christ was speaking in terms His disciples could understand,—of this world as we know it. This world is but a speck, a mere grain of sand in comparison with other worlds and other systems. Christ might have added, "What shall it profit a man if he gain the universe and lose his life?" It is only the Bible that computes the value of life in the highest of all known terms.

2. Extent.

It is a very solemn thought that whereas every man has his beginning, he has no end. His eternity must be spent somewhere. Man is the only creature in the universe outside of the angels to whom the words "eternal" and "everlasting" have any significance. How much time men spend discussing trivial matters. The weather, the style, the customs are things which change constantly. Yet human creatures are the only ones in all God's universe who have a right to use those words "eternal" and "everlasting" because they do not apply to anything else in the visible universe.

McCabe, in *The End of the World*, lengthens out the ages of the suns and planets into millions of years, but with the pessimism which ultimately overtakes all evolutionists he finds an end to it all. Only man is eternal, and he must live on after the gigantic suns of the universe have quenched their light in the ashes of their undoing.

3. Possibilities.

a. *Life contains an infinite capacity for knowledge.*

The wisest and best of men have never passed beyond the rudiments of the kindergarten of this earth. The human infant is the most helpless of all infants, but mark the gigantic strides by which he rises in a few years to such wonders of intelligence. He dives into the hidden mysteries of nature, calculates the distance of the stars, and discovers a storehouse of knowledge. But the more a man knows the less he finds he knows and the more he wants to know. The wisest men of today are only in the kindergarten of eternity's school. Here memory fails. Here questions must remain unanswered. But beyond this realm of obscurity every doubt shall be cleared away. Man shall know every secret of the earth, the sea and the heavens. "Now we know in part, but then shall we know even as we are known." Life is knowledge.

b. Life contains an infinite capacity for freedom.

The world at best is only a prison cell. We have yet to experience the freedom of the universe. Colton calls our present existence the "jailer of the soul in the filthy prison of earth, with death its only deliverer." In this world we are confined, as it were, within the walls of a narrow cell. Above us is a little window through which now and then we get glimpses of a great universe outside. The Bible is the little window which opens to us the infinite possibilities of the immortal soul, liberated from the bondage of sin and the prison house of earth. "Ye shall know the truth," Christ said, "and the truth shall make you free." Life is freedom.

c. Life contains an infinite capacity for possession.

Men covet the world and things of the world for a possession, but what trifles are these in comparison with the immense, immeasurable creation beyond. Earth is but a grain in the mountain of existence, a drop in the ocean of creation. The withdrawal of a penny from the millions in a bank would be of more consequence than the obliteration of the earth from the universe. And yet these countless suns and systems, this majestic starry universe is reserved as an inheritance for the sons of God. "He that overcometh shall inherit all

things, and I will be his God and he shall be my son."
Now we have the promise, "All things are yours," but
soon we shall have the possession. Life is possession.

d. Life contains an infinite capacity for power.

Men lust for power and are constantly struggling
upon this earth for some larger place of influence. But
even when they subdue nature, harnessing its lightnings
and utilizing its winds and waves, their forces are insignificant compared with the irresistible power this
globe exerts in traveling one second through space. It
is estimated that in a single instant the earth produces
more power than one million Niagaras in one million
years. Even when man sways his scepter, when he
commands his hosts and rules the nations, he does not
possess a fraction of the power exerted by a single
orb of the universe. Men cannot withstand the power
of the sun at a distance of ninety millions of miles,
and yet the sun is the nearest and one of the most
insignificant of the ten billion members of the stellar
universe. What is earthly power when a Joshua may
command the sun and moon to stand still for the glory
of God and the accomplishment of His purpose? "Oh,
God, thou art terrible out of thy holy places; the God
of Israel is he that giveth strength and power unto his
people." "He that overcometh and keepeth my works
unto the end, to him will I give power over the nations."
Life is power.

e. Life contains an infinite capacity for happiness.

How much joy we get in this world out of friendships,
books and the many delights in the realm of nature.
Still all the joys of the present do not test the capacity
of the soul. There are better and more permanent
things yet to come. There is no state of ecstasy on

earth that will thrill us as the Master's, "Enter thou into the joy of thy Lord." Here joy is mingled with sorrow and tears must dim the happiest face. But unspeakable, unexperienced, unending joy remaineth for that blessed place where sin, suffering and sorrow are unknown. Our present happiness is frequently terminated by our limitations. We haven't strength, we haven't means, we haven't time to pursue the things which bring us happiness. But there is a day coming when there will be time and strength and freedom for every study and every journey and every love. Life has this gracious expectation: "Thou wilt shew me the path of life; in thy presence is fullness of joy; at thy right hand there are pleasures forevermore." Life is happiness.

---

1. Give three reasons why life is so important.
2. What estimate did God put upon life?
3. What was Christ's unanswered question? (Matt. 16:26.)
4. Look up the number of times this question is found in the Gospels.
5. What do we mean by "eternal life"?
6. How does God's eternity differ from man's?
7. What does the Bible teach as to the end of the earth? (2 Peter 3:10.)
8. Name five great capacities that life contains for the immortal soul.

II

THE IMPORTANCE OF CHILD LIFE

MAN is different from the lower animals. He has a lengthened infancy. Most animals mature shortly after birth, but an infant passes through a long drawn-out period of dependence and preparation. In fact, man lives three lives during his earthly existence, each with its distinctive characteristics and requirements:

> The Child Life - - 1 to 12 years.
> The Adolescent Life, 13 to 24 years.
> The Adult Life - - 25 years up.

These periods have their marked peculiarities. At no time are the senses as keen or the memory as clear as during the child life. A child of six has just as quick perception as a man, and the memory powers of ten will never be surpassed. At no time are there as many criminals made or converts won as during the adolescent age. The adult life, while distinct from the child life and the adolescent life, is wholly built upon the foundation of this early period. Harrower says that no ideas can become the permanent possession of the world which do not first enter through the door of childhood. By the age of three, parents have done more than half of what they will ever do for their child.

Despite man's lengthened infancy and the large part it contributes to his well being, no period of life is so quickly forgotten nor so shamefully neglected as the child life. That old pagan philosopher, Socrates, used to say that if he could get to the highest point in Athens he would lift up his voice and proclaim, ''What mean ye, fellow citizens, that scrape every stone to get wealth together and take so little care of your children to whom ye must some day relinquish it all?'' ''You English,'' said King Khama, ''take great care of your goods but you throw away your children.''

That the child life is important must be recognized from the following facts:

1. Christ was a child.

He might have become flesh and dwelt among men as a mature adult, but he saw fit to pass through the long preparatory stages of infancy and adolescence and finally emerge into His comparatively short period of adult life. Christ represented the ideal of childhood and sanctified forever all that pertains to it. By birth He was of Jewish race, and among the Jews especially, children are appreciated, loved and nurtured with the utmost care for their place and part in life. ''In no denomination,'' says Rabbi Green, ''does the religious training of children take a higher place than among the Jews.'' The Jews never neglected any child. This one factor is the key to their supremacy. So writes one of our modern social psychologists, and it is true. When Josephus argued against Apion he said, ''Our principal care of all is to educate our children.'' And in the Talmud, the ancient book of Jewish wisdom, it is written, ''By the breath of the children the world is preserved.'' This was the attitude toward children with which Jesus came naturally into contact.

2. Christ magnified child life.

We are in the habit of calling upon children to follow the example of their elders. Christ did just the opposite.

a. He put the child and not the adult in the center of the group.

He did not say to the little child, "Look at Peter, what a fine fisherman he is. I trust that you will grow up and some day be like Peter. Here is Matthew. He is a successful banker. I hope that some day you will know as much about banking as Matthew." Instead of pointing to the elders as an example He pointed to the child and said, "Except ye become as little children." Our Lord never taught the child to be as a man, but He taught men to become like children.

b. He rebuked the disciples when they argued that adults had prior claim to His time.

When mothers brought their children the disciples remonstrated: "The Master is busy. He has many cares. The adult population need him. There is no time for children." But Jesus said, "Suffer the little children to come unto me and forbid them not." He seems to have had a prophetic vision of a later day when the interests of adults would claim almost exclusively the attention of the church for He says, "Take heed that ye despise not one of these little ones; for I say unto you, that in heaven their angels do always behold the face of my Father which is in heaven." These empyreal, eternal creatures are the guardians of the little ones whom man is prone to despise and neglect.

c. He emphasized the place and importance of child training in the church.

In His last charge to Peter He commissioned him to "feed my lambs." The pathos of life for Christ was that all men had begun as little children, near to God, close to His heart, but had wandered away from the road into sin. This was the intent of the parable of the lost sheep. A study of the context would indicate that it was a wandering lamb for which the Good Shepherd left the ninety and nine and searched the mountains. It is not the will of God "that one of these little ones should perish."

> "Open the door for the children,
>   Tenderly gather them in,
> In from the highways and hedges,
>   In from the places of sin.
>
> Some are so young and so helpless;
>   Some are so hungry and cold;
> Open the door for the children,
>   Gather them into the fold."

3. The child life ministers to mankind.

a. Children are the builders of the home.

The home is not only necessary for children, but in the truest and strictest sense children are necessary for the home. The birth of a baby acts strongly as a deterrent to wrongdoing in the life of the parents. Its very dependence forces them to larger usefulness. The trustful spirit of the young child is one of the most beautiful things in the world. There is no compliment that a parent can receive like the upturned face of a child speaking wonder and confidence. His implicit faith disseminates doubt and furthers the mutual faith of husband and wife.

b. Children are the builders of society.

Their existence, helplessness and need become a strong

argument for co-operation and peace in community life. These are the facts of history, that child life has been a large contributor to the peace and uplift of a community. "It is the child that keeps the world sweet and hopeful. Without childhood the race would drift into pessimism and hatred and despair."

c. *Children are the religious leaders of mankind.*

How often God has spoken to unbelieving parents through a little child. You remember the story of that atheist whose little girl had attended Sunday-school and he was somewhat distressed. So one day he wrote on a piece of paper, "God is nowhere." But the little child couldn't understand it. She had not been taught that way. She took the slip of paper and spelled it by dividing part way, "God is now here," and it led to that man's conversion.

As a pastor I never found an unbelieving father or mother who refused to have their child placed on the cradle roll of the Sunday-school. Sir George Adam Smith, when he was in Palestine, saw a shepherd carrying a lamb. He asked if it had broken a leg or if it were tired. The shepherd replied that there was nothing the matter with it. The lamb was strong and healthy, but he pointed to an old sheep trotting at his side and said, "That is the mother. She has the habit of wandering. The only way I can keep her with the flock is by taking her lamb and carrying it." Many times God has spoken through some little child whom He has taken away from its sorrowing parents. Truly, "A little child shall lead them."

4. The child life is plastic.

There is no more important law than the law of habit. A habit can almost be said to be a fixed part of us, an established fundamental of our life. It is very hard to get rid of a habit. Dr. Woolston in his object talks shows this difficulty by a play upon the word itself. He erases the "h" and still has "abit." Then he takes away "a" and has "bit" left. Finally he eliminates the "b" and still has "it." Perhaps that forcibly illustrates the tenacity of habit. "Education," says James, the great psychologist, "is the organization of acquired habits of conduct and tendencies to behavior."

Habits, physical, intellectual and moral, are generally acquired in childhood. Habits such as prayer, Bible reading, Christian observances, are also the result of religious discipline. These may be formed in every period of life, but when developed after maturity they must contend perpetually against a mob of contrary habits which persist until the end of life. Formation of habit, then, is vastly easier than reformation. By the age of thirty an individual has fashioned the groove in which his life will run. From this time ninety-nine one hundredths of all a man does he does automatically.

The child is wax to receive and granite to retain. A university professor, in giving up men in order to teach boys, gave as his reason, "If you were to write your name on brick so that it would remain, would you write it before or after it was baked?"

---

1. In what respect is man different from the lower animals?
2. What are the three life-periods of the individual?
3. How do you explain the fact that child life is so largely neglected in civilized countries?
4. What was the testimony of Socrates along this line?
5. Give four reasons why child life is important.
6. What was the Jewish attitude toward child life?
7. State three ways in which Christ magnified the importance of child life.
8. In what three ways do children minister to mankind?

9. Do you know of any instance in which an adult was converted through the instrumentality of a child?
10. When do we form our habits?
11. Why is habit formation so much easier than habit reformation?
12. Why is it more profitable to teach boys than men?

III

THE IMPORTANCE OF CHILD STUDY

C HILD study may be defined as an examination of the laws governing the growth of a personality. It involves:

1. Knowledge of a person.

No one can introduce God to an individual life unless he knows that life. The successful medium must

a. *Know God.*

That is more than to know *about* God. I know about the President of the United States, but I could not introduce him to you because I do not know him personally. If I am to successfully introduce two persons, I must know them both and I must know them well. We cannot introduce God unless we are on speaking terms with Him. It is not sufficient to have known God some time ago. We must know Him intimately and be in constant communication with Him in order to introduce Him.

b. *Know man.*

One must study man and become acquainted with him in order to know him. In the business world the successful salesman is the one who knows human nature and understands the approach to men's minds. He must study the men to whom he is selling his goods. It is the same in the religious world. We must know those to whom we are introducing God, and we find that many men fail at this point. Some men go to one extreme. They live close to God in fastings, prayer and devotion, they spend hours studying their Bible, but they do not become acquainted with men. Their usefulness to a large extent is limited. Then we find those who go to the other extreme. They know men, they are men among men, but they do not keep close to God, and their ministry also is curtailed. No Christian worker can be useful in introducing God to mankind unless he knows God and knows men.

We must know not only boys and girls but we must know *the* boy and *the* girl with whom we have to deal. Most boys and girls are better students of human nature than their teachers. They may not always get their lessons, but they study their teachers sufficiently to know just when they will be called upon to recite. We should study the child as he studies us, for only in that way can we ever hope to find an entrance into his life. "The child mind," says Patterson Dubois, "is a citadel that can be taken neither by stealth nor storm, but there is a natural way of approach and a gate of easy entry always open to him who knows how to find it."

2. Knowledge of a law.

Dr. G. Stanley Hall was one of the first to point out that life is under the control of certain laws which are practically universal and unchangeable. Child study then has a basis in facts. It investigates the facts in human development, studies the natural order of growth, and determines the modifying effect of various conditions and activities in different stages.

This law, however, needs to be qualified by our recognition of the government of a personal God. God is above law, and can and does change law. Such changes are called miracles. A miracle is an event taking place outside of nature and brought about by the special intervention of God. While a miracle is possible, it is not probable. God never works miracles to relieve men of their common sense. We may easily be guilty of the sin of presumption, in believing that God will change a law we have ignored. We have no right to close our eyes to facts with the hope that God will later on bless our ignorance and our carelessness by overruling natural laws.

From this law we conclude that

a. Life can be planned.

The mother of Theodore Cuyler refused the gift of a law library from her brother with this remark, ''Theodore is going to be a minister.'' He was only three years old at that time, but his mother believed his life could be planned. It was planned, and Theodore Cuyler became an eminent clergyman.

The success of the Catholic church lies in their firm belief that the religious life can be planned. During the days of the Reformation, when Protestantism threatened to sweep Romanism from the face of Europe, Ignatius Loyola and Francis Xavier conceived the plan of reaching after the children and rearing up a new generation of lovers and defenders of Rome. Their effort was crowned with signal success, and the triumphant advance of Protestantism was arrested by the child-reaching and the child-teaching activities of the Jesuits. The church of Rome never forgot this lesson, and to this day in the attention they give to early religious training they reiterate the immortal words of Xavier, ''Give me the children until they are seven and any one may have them afterwards.''

b. Tragedies may be prevented.

We speak of human tragedies, but, alas, we do not investigate their cause as we ought. If an engineer is called upon to build a bridge, does he build it carelessly, indifferently, with haphazard measurements and estimates? Oh, no! With his blue prints and pencil he very carefully calculates the material required to build the bridge in order that it may be able to support the stream of human lives that will pass over it. If there is a catastrophe and the bridge gives way, we hold the engineer responsible.

Think of the large number of human lives over whom no one labors with pencil and paper. When there is no blue print prepared, no care taken about the building of a life, the most natural thing in the world is a catastrophe. Someone is responsible for that human tragedy. The late Vice-President Marshall said: "If we are to teach a child nothing about right living we have no reason to complain if he goes wrong. It is not his fault, it is our neglect."

c. There is hope in formation and regeneration, but not in reformation.

The grace of God can give a repentant man a new heart, but it does not give him a new body and a new mind. It does not restore the lost opportunities of childhood.

(1) Life's mistakes cannot be wholly rectified.

You may be familiar with the story of the boy who told so many lies that at last his father required him to drive a nail into a post every time he said anything which was not true. The boy drove nail after nail into the post until the father said, "This will never do, we must find a way to remove the nails. Every time you are tempted to lie and tell the truth instead, you may pull out one of the nails." The boy put up a great fight and one after another the nails came out until one day they were all gone. Then his father said, "My boy, you must be very happy today. There are now no nails in the post." But the boy began to cry. "Oh, father, the nails are gone but the nail holes remain." We cannot eradicate the marks of sin even though forgiven.

(2) Our business is to bring a cargo and not a derelict into port.

When that boat sets sail across the ocean, has it been built merely for a calm sea or have we guarded against a possible storm? Do we care whether it reaches the other side, whether the cargo is safe? Is not every precaution taken to build that boat so that it can weather the storm?

Are we going to send the child out across the sea without any protection against the storms of life that are bound to come and beat against it, interfere with its progress and perhaps overwhelm it? How much more important is it to see that the child is adequately prepared from the beginning for a safe arrival in the haven of adult life. Eighty-seven per cent of adult converts fall away within five years, but not more than forty per cent of child converts, in the same time.

(3) Life's success depends upon obedience to God's laws.

Such obedience is not to begin late in life, but at the very start. That is the only assurance we have of success. During the World's Sunday School Convention at Tokyo, William Henry Goodwin, delegate and speaker, made the significant statement, that he owed his success in life to the practice of the principles embodied in a single verse of Scripture. Mr. Goodwin is recognized through his development of the Goodwin Stores, Limited, of Montreal and Toronto, as one of Canada's leading men of industry, and it is interesting to note just what verse of the Bible had so much to do with the making of this master merchant. It is found in Joshua 1:8: "This book of the law shall not depart out of thy mouth; but thou shalt meditate therein day and night, that thou mayest observe to do according to all that is written therein; for then thou shalt make thy way prosperous, and then thou shalt have good success."

Life's success then depends upon obedience to God's law, and obedience from the very beginning of life. This is what He says (Deut. 6:6-9): "These words, which I command thee this day, shall be in thine heart; and thou shalt teach them diligently unto thy children, and shalt talk of them when thou sittest in thine house, and when thou walkest by the way, and when thou liest down, and when thou risest up. And thou shalt write them upon the posts of thy house, and on thy gates." Again (vv. 2, 3), "Fear the Lord thy God, to keep all his statutes and his commandments, which I command thee . . . that thy days may be prolonged . . . in the land that floweth with milk and honey." There is the promise of long life, but it required that there be teaching and obedience of the Word of God from the beginning. It was to be the subject at breakfast and the topic of the evening meal. It was to be written upon the walls of the house and to be found everywhere in the home, if success was to be assured. Children were to be constantly nourished with the Word of God.

3. Knowledge of development or growth.

Those who have observed a gardener working with his flowers will understand the place that growth takes in the human life. The gardener does not create the plants. He does not enlarge or beautify. He is neither a builder nor an artist. All power of development lies within the plant, but the gardener knows the laws of the plant world and the laws of the individual flower. He knows the amount of sunshine and moisture required for the unfolding of every blossom, and he is ever watering, trimming and training the tender plant that in due time it may come in its own power to a perfect state of foliage and fruitage.

The life of a child unfolds like a flower. Within itself there is a hidden power or activity with which we have to reckon. Sun and rain and earth cannot make a plant grow if it does not use its own mysterious inner force. And no sort of influence can affect the life of a child if the child does not continually respond to it. This leads us to observe the real work of the parent or the teacher.

a. It is not to mold plastic clay.

True, the child life is plastic. He is sensitive to impressions and is storing up organized experiences which will constitute centers of interest for years to come, but an impression to be permanent must be accepted and utilized. This necessary response lies within the will of the child.

b. It is not to preserve from evil.

It is true that "babies mean this blundering human race has another chance to try again," but in their earliest hours children have tendencies away from as well as toward God. We cannot shield them from the temptations that are common to man.

c. It is not to teach little men.

If child study has accomplished any one thing during its brief history, it has proved that the child is not an adult in miniature either physically or mentally, but a different being. Children are not merely men of smaller stature. They have characteristics, physical and mental, peculiar to themselves. According to President Burritt, "Children differ from adults in powers of endurance and in the physiological processes of circulation and respiration. They have their own peculiar ways of thinking and feeling. They are concerned with the immediate and near. They are not easily moved to self-denial to secure some future blessing. They are concerned with the concrete, not with the abstract. Justice, mercy and truth as qualities, are quite beyond them, but they do understand and appreciate these qualities clothed in living personalities." We have made a great mistake in regarding the child as an immature adult. He is entirely different and separate, and we should neither feel discouraged because of his failures, nor unduly elated because of his accomplishments. There is much for us to know about him and much for us to do for him.

d. It is to build a life.

This is not the task of a day, a month, or even a year. It will occupy all of childhood and adolescence. It will not be the task of one teacher. Mother, father, kindergarten, primary, junior, grade, high school—a whole company of teachers will each perform their part in the construction of this human edifice. Every year and every teacher will make some contribution, but the completed structure will rest largely upon what the builders have done in

(1) Determining a Christian.

Winning to Christ and His work is too important and too extensive a task for any teacher to claim absolute responsibility. All teachers are in one sense of the word evangelists. Even adult converts repeatedly testify to a godly mother's contribution. The teachers in the Beginners and Primary departments are introducing the little child to the "good news" and thus leading them toward Christ. The Junior teacher is storing his mind with precious truths about the Saviour that in the last years of childhood he may diligently inquire, "What must I do to be saved?" The Intermediate and Senior teachers reap the harvest of the personal work of the evangelists that have preceded them, and if they do not have the particular part of bringing the pupil to a definite decision for Christ they will be responsible for preparing the saved to save others. Successful evangelism is built upon a deeper foundation than a "special meeting," and the far-reaching effects of a "decision day" will depend largely upon the Christian nurture of subsequent teachers.

(2) Developing a personality.

While the life and action of the child must be molded, the teacher must secure on the part of the child the operation of the will back of the action. The child should be helped so that it will act of its own initiative. *It must be brought to co-operate with the teacher.* It is this initiation of action on the part of the child that gives him personality, and it is the development of this personality that is so important in order that the temporal and eternal decision he must make will be his own.

(a)   This applies to the material world.

The end of the school teacher is not to impart knowledge. Education is not the acquisition but the use of knowledge. The word "teacher" comes from *taecem,* an Anglo-Saxon word meaning to show how to do. The word "education" comes from the Latin *educo* —to lead out. The purpose of the teacher then is to draw out and show how to do. In the drawing out of the will and action of the child upon the knowledge that has been imparted, we have the development of a personality. This is important when we realize that the progress of the world is made through its personalities. Spillman says, "The life and history of every race is written in the biographies of its personalities."

(b)   This applies to the religious world.

Christianity is a personal religion. It is centered in a Person. It makes its appeal not to a group but to an individual person. The end of the Sunday-school teacher then, is not merely to impart Bible knowledge. It is not even to make the child a Christian. No one can make any person a Christian. God must speak personally to him. The Holy Spirit must work personally with him. If he accepts Christ it will be entirely a personal matter. Thus it is supremely necessary that the personality of the child be developed that he may act rightly in this all important matter, not because we earnestly desire it, or because he sees others taking this step, but because his own will responds to the personal appeal of God.

---

1. What is the definition of child study?
2. What are the two requirements of a successful medium?
3. How do we know that boys sometimes use their teacher as a study in psychology?
4. What evidences can you give that life can be planned?

5. Is the teaching emphasis of the Catholic church scriptural?

6. Why is someone generally responsible for human tragedies?

7. Give three reasons why formation rather than reformation of character should be our objective.

8. What Bible references can you give to prove that success in life is dependent upon obedience to God's law?

9. What Bible references emphasize early religious training?

10. In what respect is the work of the gardener and teacher alike?

11. Show why children are not adults in miniature.

12. What is the real task of the parent or teacher?

13. What is the original meaning of the words "educator" and "teacher"?

14. Show how human events are related to the development of personalities.

15. Explain why the propagation of Christianity is dependent upon the development of personalities.

IV

SOURCES OF CHILD STUDY

ORGANIZED, systematic, scientific study of children is but a thing of yesterday. The reading of history must convince us that children as such had small place in the thought of writers. Child life has never been held in proper regard. Even such attention as was paid children in earlier times seems to have been with the thought of what the child was to become rather than what he was in himself. As a student in this subject wrote for an apology: "Formerly, I had the idea of probably hundreds of others, that children were not supposed to know much and we could not be expected to bother with them until they knew more." With adults childhood was tolerated because it led to manhood and womanhood. Its own beauty and glory were little understood or appreciated.

There are four sources of child study which are accessible to every student:

1. Observation.

This was the method of Pestalozzi, whose findings revolutionized the teaching methods of his day and laid the foundation of modern pedagogy. Since children may be seen doing such a great variety of things in so many different ways, innumerable opportunities are provided for observing and interpreting juvenile conduct. It is one of the best methods if the student can keep in the background and permit the child to be natural and totally unconscious of being observed. The one who does it continually will soon find himself thoroughly in love with his task. One reason why the mother is the greatest of teachers is because she has profited from her many hours of observation in the home laboratory. But such a study should include the neighborhood children that there may be opportunity for comparative investigation. All parents and teachers should frequently visit the playground for the wealth and variety of knowledge that it affords. An hour a day among the children with pencil and notebook will soon provide enough information for a valuable paper.

2. Reminiscence.

The father who has not forgotten what he was like when he was a boy, and the mother who has kept a diary of her girlhood days, are well fitted to understand their children. Unfortunately adults have so completely molded their childish traits that they would not recognize themselves as they were if an exact reproduction of their own child life could be furnished. There is nothing that we forget so quickly as our younger days. We are as children ever forgetting that which is behind and reaching forward to that which is before, so those years are forgotten in anticipation of what lies beyond. Thus it is that many a parent cannot understand his child because he cannot remember what he thought and what he did at that age. In later life we have a better recollection of our childhood days. The man who has passed into the eighties may forget many of the events of his life but vividly recalls what happened when he was a boy.

3. Literature.

Many writers have given careful study to child life and have provided excellent interpretations in their literary works. We insist that writers be true to nature. Because of this, our best authors take time to investigate carefully their subject. If a man is going to write a book about Japan, naturally he would visit the Orient and study the Japanese. If he is to write about the colored people he would study their environment and their dialect that he might write authentically. Now there are authors who have specialized in the study of child life and their productions give us a splendid interpretation of it. Such books as Stevenson's *A Child's Garden of Verses*, Riley's *After Whiles*, Tarkington's *Penrod*, and Pater's *The Child in the House*, are very helpful. The reason that such a publication as the *Youth's Companion* has retained its place and popularity for over a century is because its editors have wisely limited its pages to such contributions as reflect the writer's knowledge of adolescence.

4. Science.

The study of children by the methods of modern science has now been seriously undertaken. The fact that child life is governed by law makes it possible to compile statistics, compare conditions, and apply scientific methods to revealed knowledge that authentic conclusions may be reached. And nothing but the most systematic, unbiased, painstaking and persistent study of facts will suffice for what is classified as scientific knowledge. The validity and value of this knowledge will depend upon careful and constant research in the acquisition of all information. To be a scientist or even a student of a science, one must have an attitude of open-mindedness and a willingness to yield for the time being all opinions, prejudices and preconceived notions relative to the subject. The true scientist does not boast of his theoretical knowledge, but humbly awaits the disclosure of such conclusive evidence as in child study would require the investigation of the largest possible variety of children under the largest possible variety of conditions.

----

1. What are the four sources of child study?
2. Suggest several authors whose writings reflect a close study of child life.
3. From what source of child study have you drawn the most of your material?
4. What are the requisites for a scientific study of this subject?

V

THREE FORCES IN LIFE BUILDING

PROF. H. H. HORNE, in his *Idealism in Education*, names three important forces that operate in the building of life, heredity, environment and will. Since the latter force is so vitally associated with personality it would seem preferable to use that term instead of "will." These three forces combine in the making of each individual life. Heredity bestows capacity. Environment provides opportunity. Personality recognizes capacity and improves opportunity. As Horne so clearly puts it, "The child is born in part, he is made in part, in part he makes himself." So important are these contributions to the unfolding life that it will be well to consider them in detail.

1. Heredity.

Every child is born into the world with racial and family characteristics which are transmitted to him by his immediate and more remote ancestry. According to authorities, a child inherits one-half of his characteristics from the two parents, one-fourth of his characteristics from the four grandparents, one-eighth of his characteristics from the eight great-grandparents.

The operation of the force of heredity will be seen in the law of filial regression. The illustration of height is best understood. If both parents are unusually tall their children as a rule are taller than the general average but shorter than themselves. That is because of the influence of a grandparent or a great-grandparent. On the other hand if both parents are excessively short in stature, the children will be taller than their parents but shorter than the average. The influence of heredity may also be seen in the law of longevity. Insurance companies call this the "expectation of life." They determine the approximate life of an individual by taking the age of his father, mother, and four grandparents and dividing it by six.

Children take after their parents in energy, ability to learn and other original mental traits as they do in form, feature and physical resemblance. In the consideration of the force of heredity there are three observations to be made.

a. Children inherit tendencies, not character.

A child does not inherit the knowledge of music, but an ear, an interest and a zeal for its acquirement. A child does not inherit an appetite for strong drink, but a constitutional weakness that he may be easily led or easily discouraged. A child does not inherit tuberculosis, but may inherit tendencies to tuberculosis so that under favorable surroundings it may develop more rapidly than with some others. If nature is not kind she is at least impartial. "If a satyr cannot become a saint, neither can a drunkard reproduce his kind by heredity." Except for certain racial, physical poisons which are transmissible by infection, the child begins life with the same capacity with which his father and mother started.

b. Heredity is determined by grandparents rather than parents.

In Exodus 20:5 we read that the iniquity of the fathers shall be visited upon the children unto the third and fourth generation. There is an application of this law in all families. The wicked King Ahaz had a righteous son but a wicked grandson. The good King Hezekiah on the other hand had a wicked son but his great-grandson was one of the godliest of the twenty kings of Judah. Paul declared that Timothy owed his faith to his grandmother Lois as well as his mother Eunice.

We are not responsible for all that we have received from our ancestry, but we are responsible for what we hand down through the gates of birth. We can fulfill many of our hopes for children who shall come after us, by marriages in which physical, mental and spiritual characteristics will be happily and harmoniously blended. King Ahaziah had a good grandfather whose only mistake lay in permitting his son Jehoram to marry Athaliah, the daughter of Jezebel, the notoriously wicked wife of King Ahab. Up to this time the kingdom of Judah had preserved the purity and religion of its rulers. But this contamination was the beginning of a long series of sins and sorrows which was not ended until the house of Ahab had been entirely exterminated. Through this unwise marriage one woman, Jezebel, was permitted to bring into the royal family of Judah evil and bloodshed which was to remain for three generations.

c. Heredity is more marked in adolescence than in childhood.

After the twelfth year a thousand voices of the past make themselves heard. Unexpected likenesses in body, mind and character to parents and grandparents emerge. The stamp of the race and family is put upon form and face. A child who has hitherto resembled his mother may now reveal that he has the characteristics of his father or his father's family. The period of adolescence, then, is not only the time for the discovery of the gifts of heredity, but for the confirmation or correction of tendencies which will then manifest themselves.

2. Environment.

Environment like heredity is something of which the child is the recipient. He is helpless. The parent is the recipient of the helps or hindrances handed down to him as the heritage of his ancestry. He cannot repeal the law of his forefathers, but the parent can counteract or countenance the voices of the past in the environment he furnishes for his child. Grandparents may provide capacity. Parents primarily are responsible for environment.

There is no more important factor in the formation of life than

a. The home.

Not only does the home have exclusive control of the power of heredity, but it furnishes the environment for the most impressionable years of life. Children are molded by the sentiments, opinions and moral standards which prevail where they live and eat and sleep. Imitation comes first and comprehension later. Habits of life and attitudes of mind need to be fixed before there can be full understanding. The home is the hothouse in which the tender plant is to be shielded and shaped during its most susceptible years. It is the inalienable right of the child to be loved, to be understood, and to be educated. The home should be the guarantee that these child rights will be recognized and realized.

The home cannot delegate its task to the community. As President Forbush points out, "A school teacher not only learns to judge a given home by the kind of child who comes from that home, but she recognizes the limitations of the possibilities either of neutralizing or lessening the influence of that home." The home must not expect the school to alter materially the child's personal habits, or the church to revolutionize his ideals. "The home is the only institution," says Miss Lynch, "that is in itself strictly an educational institution. The church and the school can each help but the home and the home only, can educate." It is in the home children get their first and most enduring ideas of God. Not so much in the street as in the family. Not so much at school, as from the mother. Not what they hear in church, but what they see in their father.

Home environment depends upon:

(1) The mother.

Napoleon was once asked what France most needed. The reply of this great man who was a statesman as well as a soldier, was, "Mothers." Lincoln was universally regarded as a self-made man, yet he said, "All that I am or hope to be I owe to my mother." When asked the secret of his success, Timothy Dwight replied, "I had the right mother."

During the most impressionable years of life the mother is the child's constant companion and almost his only teacher. From her he acquires the materials for the construction of his moral and spiritual nature. The very presence and example of a mother constantly exerts a stimulating and elevating influence. Righteousness does not come by nature but by precept and practice. Juvenile delinquency follows a mother's ignorance or negligence during the habit-forming days of early childhood.

Because of the enduring character of early impressions

a mother's contribution increases with compound interest. The influence of a mother is frequently recorded in Scripture. Ammon and Absalom, who turned out so disastrously, were the sons of David's heathen wives. Solomon and Nathan were brought up in the same family and had the same father, but good mothers. Ahaz, the father of Hezekiah, was a most corrupt king. He established all the abominable practices of heathen worship and even compelled his son to walk through the fire. Likewise the grandson of Ahaz in his long reign of fifty-five years was noted for his wickedness and idolatry. How then do we explain the extraordinarily good reign of Hezekiah between two notoriously bad kings? The answer is found in his mother, Abijah. She was not the daughter of a heathen king or an unscrupulous woman. Thus we see the tremendous influence of a mother, not only upon an individual but upon a nation. Truly "the hand that rocks the cradle rules the world," and a good mother is of more consequence than the conqueror of a kingdom.

(2) The father.

The father shares with the mother an equal responsibility for the environment of the home. He particularly expresses the masculine standpoint. Through his contact with the outer world he is better able to interpret society to the children, while the mother more successfully explains the personal relations. In a well regulated family the father is a court of appeals. He is accorded a certain authority and a certain heroic quality which the mother ascribes to him in the eyes of the children. While the mother's influence is the strongest in childhood, the father's is especially prominent in the period of adolescence. To the daughter father is her first lover, to the son he should be the first hero.

The Bible clearly distinguishes between fathers who have fulfilled or failed in their responsibilities as parent. Abraham was told that his posterity would become a great and mighty nation because "he will command his children and his household after him." Eli, on the other hand, lost his prestige and priesthood because "his sons made themselves vile and he restrained them not." Paul wrote Timothy that the office of bishop or deacon should only be conferred upon a man "that ruleth well his own house."

Cheney in his *Job of Being a Dad,* and Stearns, in *The Challenge of Youth,* have revealed the neglect in the modern home through the failure of the father to function. All too frequently the father takes his responsibilities too lightly. It is very well for a man to believe that the mother can do more for their child than the father, but he has no right to expect his wife to take the place of both parents. Beginning with the adolescent period the boy will look more to the father than to the mother, and his influence upon that young life is a responsibility that no institution or government can ever assume. The great problem of the juvenile courts of America that are hearing an increasing number of crimes every year, is to find a father who is willing to be a companion and chum to the delinquent boy and girl. Any father who has a correct parental conception of the family function and an adequate parental appreciation of the possibilities bound up in his boy, will put the home in the center of his program and have all other interests subordinate. The all-important environment that will shape the years of childhood will never be properly evaluated until there is a universal recognition that the home is the world's greatest university and the father and the mother the world's greatest teachers.

b. The community.

So important is the home that all other agencies can be collected into one and set aside as auxiliary to the home and its environment. Beginning with the sixth year other agencies unite with the home in contributing to the environment of the child. Some of these operate before this time but only in a limited way and for a limited period and their influence is overshadowed by the more powerful surroundings of the home. The child may enter kindergarten, but the home, represented by his mother, takes him to the kindergarten and calls for him, so that his whole life in the kindergarten is more or less subjected to the influence of the home. It is only when the child is away for long and regular periods that its influence is neutralized by other agencies.

Some of the forces of the community that contribute to the child's environment are:

(1) The school.

The school furnishes the intellectual environment. The process of education is said to be putting the child in possession of the best heritages of the race. According to President Butler, these are natural, humanistic and spiritual. "The question How? whose answer is science, is the natural heritage. The question Why? whose answer is philosophy, is the humanistic heritage. The question Whence? whose answer is religion, is the spiritual heritage." But the public school does not attempt to answer these questions in any equal ratio. That secular education is one-sided may be seen from the statistics which proportion the contribution of the public school curriculum as follows:

80 per cent intellectual growth.
17 per cent character building.
3 per cent spiritual development.

The contribution of the public school then is almost exclusively intellectual.

(2) The church.

The church furnishes the spiritual environment. To the child the vital contribution of the church largely lies in the family pew and the Sunday-school. If the parents do not attend church or if home worship does not accompany church worship, the influence of the church is limited to the agency of the Sunday-school. Here, too, the personality of the teacher is a more powerful factor than the knowledge provided in the average Sunday-school.

(3) The gang.

The gang provides the physical and social environment. It is called a gang instead of a club because in its early days it is an unorganized group. The boy whose parents do not function in the home is more likely to depend upon some outside group to satisfy his physical and his social instincts. As the parent in the home or the teacher in the school is the controlling factor, we likewise find in the leader of the gang its governing influence. In many ways he resembles the chief of the clan in his command of a group, and the moral code of the individual member is largely determined by the public opinion of the club to which he is attached.

The combined power of heredity and environment is

illustrated in the well-known Jukes family in sharp contrast to their contemporary, the Edwards family. In the early days of our American history a coarse, lazy, vulgar man built himself a hut in the woods of central New York. In five generations he had several hundred descendants. A careful study of the twelve hundred persons who belong to the family disclosed the fact that almost without exception all were lazy, ignorant and coarse. Four hundred were physically diseased, two hundred were criminals, seven were murderers, fifty women were notoriously immoral, three hundred children died from neglect, three hundred were chronic paupers. It is estimated that these descendants of the Jukes have cost the state of New York one thousand dollars apiece.

In contrast to the Jukes family the history of the Jonathan Edwards family has been written. Out of fourteen hundred individuals, one hundred and twenty were Yale graduates, one hundred and sixty-five completed their education at other colleges; thirteen were college presidents, one hundred were college professors; more than one hundred were ministers and missionaries, one hundred were lawyers, eighty were elected to public office, seventy-five were officers in the army and navy, sixty were prominent writers, and thirty were judges.

The reason we do not have more illustrations of this character is because the forces of heredity and environment do not always operate in conjunction. Good capacity is often denied the opportunity for realization by environment, and bad tendencies are counteracted by good surroundings. Environment is man's second chance. It may confirm or correct the tendencies of heredity. This should be a source of great encouragement to parents and teachers.

3. Personality.

So far the child has not had a part in the making of his life. He has not acted, but on the contrary has been acted upon. Were he only plastic clay the laws of heredity and environment might be sufficient to construct his life. The child is more than a mere recipient. He is a reacting agent, creating his own personality by his own activity. The child comes to that condition so aptly expressed by Tennyson's "In Memoriam":

> "But as he grows he gathers much,
>   And learns the use of 'I' and 'me,'
>   And finds 'I am not what I see,
>   And other than the things I touch.'
>
> So rounds he to a separate mind
>   From whence clear memory may begin,
>   As thro' the frame that binds him in
> His isolation grows defined."

Very early in life we discover that he has a will of his own. In fact, as we have just pointed out, the child's will affects both heredity and environment. The child may improve his heredity in so far as he wills to do so. He may reject inherited musical gifts by refusing to develop them through practice. He may elect environment in so far as he wills to improve his opportunity. What a child amounts to, thus depends upon the sum total of his capacities, opportunities and will. Parents and teachers can only determine the limitations in these three directions and help the child to reach them. The child has a resisting power to all influences that act upon him, but his thwarting our efforts may even work to his advantage. Thousands of men of great natural ability have been lost to the world because they have not had to wrestle with obstacles or struggle with difficulties sufficient to stimulate their dormant powers. There is an advantage to disadvantage. Men who have

been blind or deaf or otherwise handicapped have sometimes reached a higher place in life than those who have
had the full use of all their senses. This was true of
Beethoven, the deaf musician; Prescott, the blind writer
of *The Conquest of Mexico;* Milton, whose darkened
eyes saw and who sang of *Paradise Lost;* Helen Keller,
blind, deaf and dumb, who struggling against these almost insurmountable difficulties, one day stood on the
platform and received her college diploma, seeing things
which men with eyes do not see, hearing things which
men with ears do not hear, simply because she willed it,
and the power of her personality raised her above all
obstacles and all environment.

To a large extent the child must work out his own
life as captain of his destiny. Partly we shape him and
partly he must shape himself. In childhood we may act
upon him, but in adolescence he will largely act for
himself. There are three observations to be made in
the consideration of this force.

a. Habits shape a personality.

Descartes claimed that individual thought is the evidence of a personality, but the power to think and act
individually is necessarily dependent upon the acquisition of habits of thought and action. We can form
habits of thinking and acting that will most forcibly
influence our own thought and action. Most actions are
in some degree controlled by individual thought, but the
mechanical contribution of habit is always present. It
is evident that many an action is directed by habit even
when the doer thinks that he has consciously chosen it
in perfect freedom. The drunkard never thinks that
he is in the grip of an all-powerful habit. As Professor
James puts it, "The greatest thing in all education is

making our nervous system our ally instead of our enemy. Could the young but realize that soon they will become mere walking bundles of habit, they would give more heed to their conduct while in the plastic state. We are spinning our own fates, good or evil, and never to be undone. Every smallest stroke of virtue or vice leaves its never so little scar. Man excuses every new indiscretion by saying, 'It won't count this time.' He may not count it, a kind heaven may not count it, but it is counted nevertheless. Down among the nerve cells and fibres the molecules are counting it, registering and storing it up to be used against him when the next temptation comes. Nothing we ever do is in the strictest, scientific literalness 'wiped out.' '' We acquire the larger part of our personal habits before twenty and most characters are determined by thirty.

b. Expression intensifies a personality.

We may better understand the relation of expression to the development of a personality by a study of the nervous system. Running from the brain in all directions is a double set of wires which transmit the most delicate stimuli. One of these wires is the sensory nerve. Its function is to carry communications to the brain. Paralleling it is the motor nerve which conveys the return communication from the brain. The sensory nerve receives the impression, the motor nerve returns the expression. The sensory nerve is the servant of external influences, the motor nerve is the executive of the personality. It can be readily seen then that the development of expression has a great deal to do with the making of a personality. Getting a response or a reply to our impression is an evidence of life, and an intelligent and individualistic response, the evidence of a personality. In the dark I stumble over the dog. Almost immediately there is an expression to my impression. But that yelp of the dog is not an intelligent or an individualistic expression.

Leadership will be developed in proportion to the opportunity we give in our educational program for original thought and expression. It is upon this principle that we must act if we are to develop a strong personality in the child. To continue to crowd the mind with information without giving opportunity to the child for self-activity, will produce a negative character, a man without initiative or personality. Self-made men are frequently strong personalities because circumstances have thrown them upon their own resources and drawn out their powers of expression. Many a potent personality lies dormant like the buried talent, because it has never been called into use.

c. Religion controls a personality.

It is not creeds or principles but in the last analysis a person that dominates a personality. This is true of the mother and the teacher, whose personality will have far greater weight with the child than any number of lessons, and the power of the mother's or teacher's religion lies in their worship of a superior Person. Creeds cannot command the devotion of personalities. Only a supreme, supernatural Person makes possible the phenomena of worship. The greatness of God does not rest in His omnipotence nor His omniscience. It lies in His character. There is no limit to His ability and power. The only restriction is His will. He is eminently wise and will not will what is foolish. He is eminently just and will not will what is inequitable. He is absolutely good and will not will what is evil.

Character is not so much made up of impulses as restraints. All psychologists agree as to the controlling influence of religion. To be irreligious is to say, "I will not be controlled." In passing from parent control to self-government the child is in danger of passing beyond any external control. Now when a person passes beyond external control he is an outlaw. He has no regard for the laws of God or man and he is dangerous to society. Regeneration not only recognizes God in control of the universe but of our lives. The child's faith is a surrender of will in recognition of a superior Personality who commands respect and obedience. To surrender will requires faith, but faith does not destroy personality. A person of great faith does not lose his forcible, aggressive attributes and become a passive, nonresisting being. While his powers are no longer devoted to impressing his own will on others, they are now bent to the promotion of the will of the One to whom he has surrendered his own leadership. The surrendered life is the militant, victorious life. Paul surrendered his will and that great personality conquered Europe for Christ. George Mueller surrendered to God and was enabled to provide for thousands of orphans. Charles Spurgeon surrendered to God and became the peerless preacher. D. L. Moody surrendered to God and today thousands of students receive the benefit of his life investment.

We want personality. We want to develop a personality, but the only safety in the development of a personality is having it under the control of God. A great personality may be a detriment to the community rather than a help. Fire is a great agency, but fire can be very destructive unless held under control. And so when we speak about the tremendous possibilities of a personality we must recognize that it can be just as strong and powerful for Satan and the embassies of darkness as for God and the principalities of heaven. Therefore we have to keep in mind that safety lies in the place and power that religion has in the life of all personalities.

---

1. What are the three forces in life building and what is their relation to each other?
2. Illustrate the law of filial regression.
3. How does heredity affect longevity?
4. What three observations are made in considering the law of heredity?
5. Apply the law of heredity in the case of King Ahaz and King Ahaziah.
6. How is heredity related to adolescence?
7. What is the relationship of grandparents, parents and children to heredity and environment?
8. Why is the home the most important factor in the formation of life?
9. Why is the mother the child's greatest teacher?
10. Illustrate from Scripture the far-reaching power of a mother's training.
11. Why is the father's co-operation essential in home training?
12. Name five ways in which the father can contribute to the making of an ideal home.
13. What are the three forces of the community and what does each contribute to a child's environment?
14. When is the gang most likely to exert a strong influence upon child life?
15. Illustrate the power of heredity and environment from the statistics of the Jukes and Edwards families.
16. Show how the will of a child affects both his heredity and environment.
17. Illustrate the power of will in the lives of Beethoven, Prescott and Helen Keller.
18. How do habits shape a personality?
19. What has expression to do with the developing of a personality?
20. Why is religion essential to the control of personalities?

VI

THREE PHASES OF RELIGIOUS EDUCATION

THE wise man said, "Train up a child in the way he should go, and when he is old he will not depart from it." Men who have questioned the infallible certainty of this law have not realized what is meant by the word "train." Many children have been *told*. Some have been *taught*. Few have been *trained*. Education is not merely a telling process. It is not even a teaching process. It involves training. What is the difference?

Telling is helping to know.
Teaching is helping to know and grow.
Training is helping to know and grow and do.

Many teachers are prone to talk rather than teach because they regard their task as the impartation of knowledge, so they

"Ram it in, cram it in,
  Children's heads are hollow,
Slam it in, jam it in,
  Still there's more to follow."

Education is not the acquisition but the use of knowledge. It involves growth and action.

The supreme work of Christ's ministry was not preaching or teaching, but training. The twelve disciples constituted the first teacher-training class. He gave them a three year course. He not only taught them, He lived with them and directed their life and action.

He made it a point to see that His scholars assimilated and applied His teaching. He might easily have arranged for them to meet Him at a certain hour in Jerusalem for instruction and then dismissed them that they might return to their work. But He lived with them. He entered into their life hour after hour. He ate with them, slept with them, worked with them. He was their constant companion. They developed under His supervision, not only from the information which He imparted, but because they worked out for themselves the things which He taught them. He sent out first the twelve, and then the seventy. There was a practical work department connected with this school.

Christ gave attention to the individual. Peter was Christ's most perplexing problem. He was the natural leader of the apostolic company. Jesus encouraged him and acknowledged his strength when He called him a rock. He was one of the select three whom Jesus took with Him on special occasions. It was the mother of Peter's wife whom Jesus cured of a fever. He saved him from death by drowning. He told Peter that He prayed for him. He chided him when he refused to have Jesus wash his feet, and reproved him for cutting off the ear of the high priest's servant. When Peter denied Him, He cast upon him a sad and compassionate look. After the resurrection He sought him out in person and commissioned him to shepherd others. Christ was a model teacher.

The religious training of a child is a complex and comprehensive process. It involves his intellect, his emotions, and his will. To be educated religiously he must *know*, *feel* and *do*. That a child may *know*, adequate provision must be made in the educational program for:

1. Information.

The child is born with a capacity for knowledge. From his earliest hours he begins to gather information. The function of the parent and teacher is to give him every opportunity and render him every assistance in this pursuit. A trained mind can obtain information far more readily than one that is not disciplined. For this reason a course of study is provided in the public schools for the development of the intellect. Such studies as philosophy, mathematics, science and languages are placed in the curriculum for the purpose of training the intellect as well as storing the mind with facts and ideas.

An important part of the program of religious education consists in storing the mind with facts concerning God and His Word. A child is born with a right to know God, and it is the place of the parent and teacher to see that this knowledge is provided as readily and as adequately as a knowledge of the affairs of men.

The Jews laid great emphasis upon the gathering of religious knowledge. The home, the school, the synagogue reinforced one another in the study of the Scriptures. One of their favorite maxims was, "The people which knoweth not the law is accursed." We read in Isaiah that the reason the Jews went into captivity was because they were without knowledge. Paul writes of the failure of religious zeal which is not according to knowledge. In our present program of religious education there is no lack of emphasis upon the imparting of information. The Sunday-school, which is the chief agency of religious education, devotes about ninety per cent of its time to this phase of the work. That children are not better provided with biblical knowledge is because they are not given more time.

That children do not retain more biblical knowledge is because proper attention has not been given to the other phases of religious education.

In addition to information there must be

2. Worship.

As knowledge has to do with intellect, worship has to do with emotion. Besides knowing things with the intellect, man attaches to the things he knows certain values which his intellect cannot know. Information may provide knowledge, but the development of the emotions creates appreciation. The one has to do with the head, while the other has to do with the heart. The absent-minded philosopher may lose all interest in fine arts because he fails to develop his world of appreciation. To prevent students from being abnormal in intellectual growth our public schools have introduced into the curriculum such subjects as music, literature and art to magnify the emotional element.

When one takes his emotions into religion it gives rise to worship and ritual. The emotions provide affection and love in religion. This was the one purpose of the ceremonial law of the Israelites. They had lived in bondage under the Egyptians for many years without knowledge of God. It was a process of education, then, by which they were not only to know God but to revere, respect and love Him. Hence we find rituals and ceremonials taught during their years of wandering in the wilderness. In fact, religion is a matter of the emotions as much as the intellect. A man can love God with all his heart even when he cannot know Him perfectly. The thirteenth chapter of First Corinthians will convince us that the understanding of all mysteries and all knowledge without love, is nothing. We speak of the importance of a rational religion, but it is interesting to note that love enters into our decisions fully as much as knowledge. All great decisions that man makes will be tempered by his affections as well as his knowledge. This is the case in his religious decisions. It was William Jennings Bryan who said, "The decisions of the heart are more to be depended upon than the decisions of the head."

A child is born with a capacity to know God, but an instinct to worship Him. Children are not born atheists and agnostics. Through neglect they become so. Paul in his sermon to the intellectual Athenians declared that all men are born with an instinct to worship and to seek after God. Because a program of information has not been provided, multitudes of pagans today, like the ancient Greeks, ignorantly worship the unknown God.

Since a child is born with the instinct of worship he must be taught to pray and to praise. Long before a child can understand God he can be taught reverence and respect by precept and example. He can see his father read from the Bible, kneel down in prayer and bow his head for the blessing three times a day. He can go with his father and mother to church. He can soon learn that Sunday is different from the other days of the week. He has begun to understand something about reverence, respect and love in his father and mother, so that when he gets older he may ask as the children asked their fathers in Israel, "What mean these things?" Then the father can explain who God is and what relation the family bears to Him. Thus worship often precedes information. The reverence that Catholics have for their priests and institutions is due to the emphasis which they put upon this phase of education in their religious life.

In the present program of the Sunday-school only six per cent of its emphasis is placed upon worship. The neglect of a program of worship is manifested in the later relations of the child or the adult to the church, such as

a. Attendance.

Why do older boys and girls, young people and adults, attend church irregularly? Why is there not that consistency about their attendance at church which marks their attendance at school or at business? They have never been trained.

b. Punctuality.

Why is it that children and adults are late to church and Sunday-school when they are not late elsewhere? They have never been trained to be punctual at God's house and in God's services.

c. Offering.

Why is it that we have so few tithers in our churches, so few regular contributors, such a large number of church members who are content to give spasmodically? Giving is a part of worship which has been neglected in their earliest years.

3. Expression.

As knowledge has to do with intellect, and worship with emotion, expression has to do with will. It has already been seen what a large place expression has in the making of a personality. The impressional side of education is giving information, but the expressional side is building a personality. Through will and action knowledge becomes a personal possession. In our public schools we have such studies as history, biology, sociology and economics to further the will and action of the individual. The value of these subjects in stimulating personal achievement has been well expressed in Longfellow's "Psalm of Life."

> "Lives of great men all remind us
> We can make our lives sublime,
> And departing, leave behind us
> Footprints on the sands of time."

The expressional side of education is allowing the pupil certain activities that develop character by doing things. It is also true that a child learns far more surely by expression than by information. Psychology teaches that a child remembers ten per cent of what he hears, fifty per cent of what he sees, seventy per cent of what he says and ninety per cent of what he does. Since he is more likely to remember what he says and what he does, we need to give attention to expressional methods. But not more than four per cent of the emphasis of the Sunday-school is placed upon expression. It is true that the young people's societies, such as Christian Endeavor and Epworth League, pay particular attention to expression, but the fact that only a small percentage of our pupils attend these sessions and the program is not correlated with the Sunday-school, tends to limit their usefulness. Pastors agree that Sunday-school scholars trained in Christian Endeavor meetings make positive and aggressive leaders.

One of the greatest problems today is the multitude of do-nothing Christians in our churches. A great mass of members do not take an active part in the work of the church. They are loafers and loiterers, contributing little or nothing to the usefulness of the church. These people are hardly to blame, because there never has been a place for expression in their training. As children they have been taught to sit still and receive, and when they become adults they continue in this passive attitude. They have never been trained to give out as they have received and thus become channels of blessing.

Christ laid great stress upon expression in His religious program. After the Sermon on the Mount He said, "Whosoever heareth these sayings of mine and *doeth* them, I will liken him unto a wise man, which built his house upon a rock," and "Everyone that heareth these sayings of mine, and *doeth* them not shall be likened unto a foolish man." "Not everyone that saith unto me, Lord, Lord, shall enter the kingdom of heaven, but he that *doeth* the will of my Father which is in heaven." James said, "Be ye *doers* of the Word and not hearers only." This was also emphasized in Christ's teaching concerning the first and great commandment. Men were to love God with all their mind, that is, all their intellect. They were also to love God with all their heart, that is, all their affection. But not the least were they to love God with all their soul, all their will and all their strength, that is, all their actions.

The parable of the good Samaritan illustrates the complete educative process of knowing, feeling and doing. The passing priest *knew* that one of his fellowmen had fallen among thieves and lay bruised and bleeding just across the road. The priest had information. The tragedy had appealed only to his intellect. Curiosity, if not compassion, prompted the Levite to go and look upon the scene of the assault. He undoubtedly felt that a brutal crime had been committed and probably cast a look of pity upon the unfortunate traveler. The Levite had information and compassion. The tragedy appealed to his emotions as well as his intellect. But the good Samaritan not only saw the helpless victim and had compassion on him, but he "bound up his wounds . . .

and *took care* of him." He *knew*, he *felt* and he *acted*. The tragedy had appealed to his intellect, emotions and will. It commanded the head, the heart and the hand. Information alone failed to accomplish anything. Even the awakening of the sympathies was not sufficient to render aid. It was knowledge quickened by love and actuated by will that produced results.

The complete educative process of knowing, feeling and doing is absolutely necessary to prepare the individual for evangelistic effort. Conversion implies more than information and feeling. Repentance requires not only a knowledge of sin and a feeling of intense sorrow for sin, but a turning from it and a turning to the only Saviour from sin.

4. The threefold program of training.

The new program of religious education calls for a combination of information, worship and expression in equal proportion. This may be accomplished in two ways.

a. *The modified Sunday-school.*

The period of the present Sunday-school in this plan would be lengthened to one and a half hours. The first half hour would be devoted to information either by study of the lesson or instruction by the teacher. It is recognized by every Sunday-school teacher that it is a difficult task to secure any study of the lesson in advance. The plan of supervised study so effectively used in the public schools could well be adopted by the Sunday-school. The second half-hour would be given over to a program of worship. For this purpose the church auditorium should be used that the surroundings may provide an atmosphere of worship. The program will include singing of children's hymns, participation in

responses and congregational prayers. A short sermon
may be preached by the pastor. The third half-hour
should be spent in recitation, discussion and expression
upon information received during the first period.
Every effort will be made at this time to draw out the
expressional powers of the child. Time will be reserved
at the close for the study assignment of the next lesson.

b. The tri-weekly church school.

This plan presupposes the organization and operation
of a week-day church school. There is an arrangement
with the public schools whereby pupils are dismissed at
certain hours so they may receive religious instruction
in their respective churches. In this week-day session
the imparting of information is the main objective.
However it includes a program of worship and hand
work suited to the lesson. The Sunday-school now becomes the second session. The lesson of the week session
is continued with special emphasis laid upon a program
of worship. Information is not excluded, but the main
emphasis is on the spirit and forms of worship. The
platform exercises are devotional and there are prayers
in the class by the teacher and pupils. The great hymns
of the church are studied and sung. On Sunday afternoon or evening the Christian Endeavor Society now
constitutes the expressional session. The topics for discussion grow naturally out of the week-day and Sunday
lessons. These expressional meetings belong to the
pupils. They carry on the meeting under the care of
a superintendent, one pupil acting as leader. They are
well prepared to express themselves upon the topic as
they have already studied it in the two previous sessions. Moreover instead of a few attending the expressional session its correlation with the week-day church

school and the Sunday-school will provide a full attendance of all the scholars.

---

1. What is the difference between telling, teaching and training?
2. Illustrate how Christ conducted His training class.
3. What are the three phases of religious education?
4. What has mental discipline to do with the gathering of information?
5. How much attention does the Sunday-school give to information?
6. Why do children retain so little Bible knowledge?
7. What have the emotions to do with religion?
8. Did Paul provide worship or information for the pagan Athenians?
9. Why should worship precede information?
10. Show how the neglect of a program of worship in the Sunday-school affects the later relations of the child to the church.
11. What are the relative values of the eye-gate and ear-gate of information compared with verbal and manual expression?
12. Compare the expressional values of the Sunday-school and the Christian Endeavor or Young Peoples' Society.
13. What passages of Scripture would indicate Christ's emphasis upon expression?
14. Illustrate the complete educative process of knowing, feeling and doing.
15. What is the modified Sunday-school?
16. What is the tri-weekly church school?

VII

THREE FIELDS OF RELIGIOUS EDUCATION

THE Jewish people are one of the greatest mysteries of the world. A nation as old and as powerful as the Chinese, but without king or country; scattered among the nations, and yet not assimilated by them; persecuted and yet prospered, they are without parallel in history. But for the key of Scripture they would ever remain the great mystery of the ages. One who has given a careful study to these peculiar people cannot help but be impressed with the prominence of religious education in their lives and its contribution to their prosperity and permanence. Josephus said of his people, "Our principal care is to educate our children, and we think it to be the most necessary business of our home life." This marked emphasis which was laid upon religious education did not escape the observation of the pagan writer Philo: "The Jews look upon their laws as a revelation from God and they are taught in these holy laws, so to speak, from their very swaddling clothes by their parents, masters and teachers." The Jews did not contribute science, philosophy or literature to the world's knowledge. Their only contribution was religion, and yet that religion was so magnified in its teaching and practice as to impress this pagan writer.

Jewish education was conducted on what is now called the intensive plan. The home, the school and the church reinforced one another. It was the continuity, co-operation and correlation of these three agencies that intensified and perfected their religious training. The home, the school and the church exist today, but their failure to function or co-operate in the religious educational program is only too obvious. Perhaps by a few comparisons the needs of the day as well as the possibilities of a correlated program, may be demonstrated. First and foremost of the three fields of religious education is

1. The home.

As we have already indicated, the supremacy of the home as an organic educational agency is due to its determination of character in both heredity and environment. The former lies wholly within its domain, and the latter is limited to its province during the most susceptible years of childhood. The religious instruction of the home, then, is of the greatest importance.

For comparison let us consider the religious education of three different homes.

a. The Jewish home.

Jewish education began with the mother. Her religious duties in connection with her household molded her children. Long before the child could go to school or synagogue the private and united prayers and the domestic rites, whether for the Sabbath or festival seasons, would indelibly impress themselves upon his mind. Her religious observance of the set feasts could not but attract his earnest attention. There was the feast of Purim, the feast of Tabernacles, the feast of Weeks, the Passover, and the Day of Atonement, occupying many days in their observance and celebration. The Jewish child could not but realize that religion was a very important thing just from the amount of time which was given to the observation of these feasts and ceremonies. His mother's religious teaching would not soon be forgotten. It was on his mother's knee that the stories of patriarchs and prophets, statesmen and warriors, poets, princes and patriots were taught to the little child. As teachers of their children women of every country may learn lessons from the mothers of Israel.

The father also made his contribution. He felt honored in having this privilege. For him to impart a knowledge of the divine law was as great a spiritual distinction as to have received it from Moses himself. To this paternal duty everything else must give way. As soon as the child could speak the father gave him his first lesson. It was the birthday text—some verse beginning with, ending with, or at least containing the letters of his Hebrew name. There were the psalms and prayers to be learned. The earliest education was given to the memorizing of Scripture.

b. *The colonial home.*

During the colonial period of our country, before the Revolutionary War, we find another home where religious instruction was paramount. It is safe to say that the Bible was used every day in the average colonial home. The husband and father was the high priest of his house. He would read to his family and cause his children to read daily from the Bible as soon as they were far enough advanced to do so. One writer of that day speaks of having read the entire Bible twelve times by the age of sixteen. The children were also required to say their prayers in connection with the general family worship. Moreover the child was taught to respect the Bible. It was a sacred volume to our American forefathers. It was the book for which they had suffered and even died. To them it was most precious and this appreciation of the Bible was stamped in the fibre of every child's heart in that day. It was not a book to be disregarded or treated carelessly and disrespectfully. It was not a book to be read if you chose and neglected if you felt like it. It was the One Book of all. Indeed historians agree that the Bible was the universal child's book of that day.

In the colonial home a religious atmosphere pervaded throughout, nor was honesty, truth and love wanting. The family was united. These indeed were happy homes. There was parental authority and home discipline. The father and mother were honored and their wishes respected. The what-do-you-think-I-am and the what-do-you-take-me-for attitude of youngsters was unknown in that day. There was almost a complete absence of crime and divorce.

c. The modern home.

What place does the Bible occupy in the average American home of today? None at all. One of our leading educators recently said, "That the Bible no longer holds the place it once did in the homes of English-speaking men and women, is a proposition that hardly needs proof." In 1914 the National Congress of Mothers and Parent-Teachers' Associations reported a "rapid progressing obliteration of family religion." Another writer, a year later, declared that family worship was so rare as to be almost phenomenal whenever found.

As for the religious atmosphere around the average American home, everybody knows that it is wanting. A few years ago the school teachers of New York City

discovered 860,000 children without any knowledge of
the Bible and void of all sense of right and wrong because there was not a vestige of Bible or Bible teaching
in their homes. The Inter-church World Movement
survey discovered twenty-seven million boys and girls
in the United States growing up without any home
training in religion. A nation which leads the world
in crimes and divorce is not likely to afford many homes
where religious training will have its proper place. The
intensive life of American people, with father in business and fraternity, and mother in club and politics, is
not conducive to the furtherance of home training.

The chief text-book of the home today is the sensational newspaper and the child's chief educator the vice,
vulgarity and violence of the movie. For religious education the parent substitutes the movie, with its dangerous fascination for the impressionable mind of the
child. We find that one week's attendance at the movies
is five times the number that will congregate at all our
numerous churches and Sunday-schools. Not only does
the child attend the movie five times more frequently,
but he learns five times more readily than in the Sunday-
school. Most Sunday-school teachers owing to lack of
training use the ear gate while the movies use the eye
gate and, as we have seen before, a child remembers
fifty per cent of what he sees but only ten per cent of
what he hears.

2. The school.

Next in importance to the home as a field of religious
education is the school. While the school cannot sup-
plant the home as an educational agency, it can supplement it. The lack of home training greatly increases
the importance of the school, because the failure of the

family must now become the function of the school if anything at all is to be accomplished.

The first schools were all religious schools. Religion was the first and foremost subject. By way of comparison let us consider

a. *The Jewish school.*

The child was sent to school at the age of five or six. Under the best trained teachers he received a graded education whose sole objective was moral and religious. Up to the age of ten the Bible was the only text-book. Teaching was the most honorable of all professions. As Prof. Hinsdale says, ''In no other country has teaching ever been so magnified as it was in Judea, and in no other nation has the teacher ever attained to such an exalted position.'' Even today the Jewish school maintains the same thoroughness that was characteristic of the school of Christ's day. No less than three hundred and twenty-five hours a year are given to daily religious instruction under well trained teachers. As a people the Jews believe thoroughly in education. Their only failure lies in the fact that not more than five per cent of their children are attending these schools. As the other 95 per cent for the most part do not attend Sunday School, it is easy to understand why such a large proportion drift into atheism and agnosticism.

b. *The parochial school.*

The parochial school has always been an important adjunct to the Catholic church. In 1884 the third council of Baltimore enacted legislation providing for a Catholic school in connection with every church. At present there are two million children attending elementary parochial schools. All Catholic education is religious education. The catechism forms the basis of all instruction. To the Catholic child religion may appear a very formal thing, but it is a very constant and a very important thing. Every Catholic school teaches religion for a definite period each day and no less than two hundred hours are provided every year. The only weakness of the parochial school from the Catholic standpoint is its failure to reach more than one-fourth of its constituency. This is largely due to the strength and excellency of our public school system.

c. The public school.

It was left for the colonists of the New England settlements to lay the foundation of our great public school system. These communities were intensely religious as well as democratic. They believed that religion was essential and that to provide instruction in religion was the obligation of the community. For that reason the three R's, reading, 'riting, and 'rithmetic, were taught to every boy and girl. The Bible for many years was the only text-book. Even when the Bible was finally discarded, the first text-books were filled with biblical material. There never was a greater text-book than the celebrated *New England Primer*. For one hundred and fifty years it was the outstanding text-book of our public school system. More than three million copies were printed. No other American text-book has ever held its place so long or been so widely used. Yet fully eighty-seven per cent of this remarkable *New England Primer* was composed of Bible selections.

Today we find that for all practical purposes the Bible has been eliminated from our public school curriculum. The Puritans thought that reading, 'riting and 'rithmetic were essential for a knowledge of the Scriptures, but today we are teaching the three R's without any recognition of their relationship to religion. Four states require Bible reading (not Bible study) in their schools. Ten states forbid the use of the Bible. In the remaining states it is optional. The first schools were centered in religion and all expenditure was made from a religious motive. Our present schools have no place for religion.

3. The church.

In the Jewish program of religious education the church never supplanted the home or the school as a field of religious training. The service of the synagogue supplemented the daily instruction of the home and school and deepened the channel that was made by the teacher's effort. The readings, prayers, psalms and sermons intensified the program of worship already inaugurated by parent and rabbi.

The Catholics likewise maintain that the Sunday-school is a mere makeshift in the process of educating children religiously and that the daily church school is absolutely essential. The responsibility of child training among Protestants has been shifted from both the home and school to the church. It is questionable whether the Protestant church through its Sunday-school will ever be able to provide for its constituency without at least the co-operation of the home and the recognition of the school. Before the church can even approach the stupendous task which Protestants have relegated to its shoulders, parents will have to see that children attend Sunday-school with as great regularity as they attend public school, while the state will have to give recognition and time for what work is carried on by the church. This is the nearest approach we can have in this day to a union of the home, the church and the state.

One would think that with the burden of religious

education now resting almost exclusively upon the
church it would regard this work of primary importance.
But such is not the case. The Protestant church has
never taken religious education seriously. It has been
the great sponsor of our splendid public school system
where religion is not taught. Vast sums of money have
been expended by the church in building and maintain-
ing colleges, but not more than two per cent of our
population enter these institutions and then in the later
adolescent period of life when religious thought and
habit have already been formed and fixed.

The failure of the church to assume its responsibility
is shown by the following facts:

a. *Churches are built and equipped for adults
rather than children.*

The type of building in the apostolic period was well
suited for the interlocutory plan of teaching. When
later the church centered about the large auditorium the
apartment building was abandoned, and it is only in
recent years that we have recognized our mistake and
provided department and class rooms for the work of
the teaching ministry.

b. *Church programs are primarily prepared for
adults.*

The choicest hours of the day are given over to the
preaching service, the Sunday-school coming before or
after. This is a service of adults for adults and by
adults. When children attend they find almost nothing
that they can understand and little that they can intelligently feel.

c. *Ministers are trained to preach rather than to
teach.*

Despite the fact that Christ was a teacher rather than

a preacher and the early church maintained that the school was the connecting link between itself and the world, it is only in recent years that our theological seminaries have provided courses in religious education. It is sad to see so much attention given to the preparation for preaching to the utter neglect of the teaching ministry.

d. The Sunday-school is inadequately financed.

The relative importance assigned religious education in the estimation of the church is emphasized in the distribution of its funds. American churches today spend $16,000,000 for the single item of music. But the pathos of it is that often where these large sums are expended for music and floral decorations the Sunday-school is not even on the budget. In fact, only too often the Sunday-school is supported by the pennies of the children. These children have even been solicited by the church to help pay off its mortgage. What would you think of a father who sent his child to work in order to support him when it was his duty to care for that child? The church owes it to her children to provide them a religious education.

e. The Sunday-school is inadequately organized and graded.

Two-thirds of the children of the country are not being reached, and those that are enrolled in Sunday-schools attend only about half the time. The children are not graded according to age, and they receive instruction in an adult lesson from an untrained and only too often, an unprepared teacher. If the Catholic church educated its youth in religious methods as carelessly as the average Protestant church, it would break down in a generation. If the public school should be no more successful in removing illiteracy than the church, two-thirds of our nation would not be able to read or write and the remaining one-third would be no further advanced than the second reader.

Considering the facts as stated, it does not seem strange that the Protestant church is addressing itself anew to the fundamental task of training children. The only amazing thing is that many churches are not awake to their responsibility and are content with conditions as they are.

The educational agencies of the church are its chief recruiting forces. Frank L. Brown, the well known Sunday-school worker, has most excellently illustrated this in his article entitled "The Sunday School as a Gold Mine." "If a business man received from one department of his business ninety per cent of his entire profits, ninety per cent of his trained workers and practically all his new business, he would pay considerable attention to that department. Especially would this be so if that department was consuming only ten per cent of his capital and time. The possibilities are that he would cut out or cut down the unprofitable departments and concentrate his capital and energy in the fruitful department. The Sunday-school is the gold mine of the church. The pastor and the people have put into its development ten per cent of the church's income, ten per cent of the time of the pastor and members, and it has yielded ninety per cent of the new members, workers and new home contacts. The dividends have a long record of steady payments. Good church strategy would suggest that the pastor and the people properly provide this enormously productive department with equipment, leadership, hard thinking and broad planning."

"If the Sunday-school activities should be suddenly and permanently terminated," says former Governor Kendall of Iowa, "I doubt if the church would survive a generation." The church must teach or die. Not only is the preservation of the church at stake, but the future of our country as well. The testimony of one hundred governors, congressmen, public and business men, as summed up in William E. Atkinson's *Value of the Sunday School*, is that the Sunday-school is among the most indispensable institutions of America and that the educational ministry to childhood is the most important task of the individual church in the present day.

---

1. Show how religious education is vitally associated with the national life of the Jews.
2. How may religious education be conducted on the intensive plan?
3. Why is the home as an educational agency far more important than the school or church?
4. What was the educational value of the Jewish festival seasons?
5. What contribution did the Jewish father make toward the training of his child?
6. Describe the colonial home and the place the Bible occupied in it.
7. What did the National Congress of Mothers and Parent-Teacher's Association report regarding family religion in the modern home?
8. How many children in New York city today are without religious education? How many in the United States?
9. Compare the influence of the movies with that of the Sunday-school.
10. What is the success and failure of the Jewish school?
11. What is the value of the parochial school?
12. What prompted the Puritan fathers to establish the first public schools?
13. What was the *New England Primer?*
14. What is the present attitude of the various states toward the use of the Bible in the public schools?
15. What is the Catholic estimate of the Sunday-school?
16. How can home, school and church be united in a program of religious education?

17. State five facts that indicate the church has never taken religious education seriously.
18. Why is the Sunday-school a gold mine?
19. What is the testimony of the leading men of America regarding the Sunday-school?

VIII

PERIODS OF CHILD STUDY

IT IS recognized by every authority that as a child develops from infancy to maturity there are certain definite periods. These periods have definite characteristics and are clearly marked. This does not mean that there are distinct boundary lines that can be fixed in any particular age. Growth is gradual and continuous. The infant becomes a child and the child becomes a youth without our realizing the precise time of transition. Sometimes new characteristics appear suddenly. Some children mature more rapidly than others. In fact individuals differ greatly, but for the most part we may look for dominant characteristics at different stages of development. These overlap from one period to another but reach the peak of their power during the period to which they are assigned.

The recognition that the unit of the modern Sunday-school is the department, and the necessity of limiting the cycle of a department lesson to three years, have determined the age groups even more than the natural boundaries of psychology. The problem of holding the adolescent in Sunday-school is a serious one, since more than half drop out during the high school age. It has been found that where the contacts of the pupils during the week are continued on Sunday, interest in the Sunday-school can be more easily maintained. Adolescents resent being grouped with children, but will respond to a plan that segregates them with those with whom they are associated during the week. For this reason pupils attending the junior high school should constitute the Intermediate department, and the young people in the classes of the senior high school should compose the Senior department of the Sunday-school. It is also much more effective to have the pupils in the Primary and Junior departments grouped according to school grade rather than age. The following plan, therefore, is to be recommended for all schools:

CHILD STUDY PERIODS	AGES	PUBLIC SCHOOL GRADES	SUNDAY SCHOOL DEPTS.
Infancy	0- 3....		Cradle Roll
Early Childhood	4- 5....	Kindergarten	..Beginners
Middle Childhood	6- 8....	I, II, III	.......Primary
Later Childhood	9-11....	IV, V, VI	......Junior
Early Adolescence	12-14....	Junior High	....Intermediate
Middle Adolescence	15-17....	Senior High	....Senior
Later Adolescence	18-24....	College	........Young People

The greatest objection to this arrangement is that the Intermediate department is now called upon to minister to both childhood and adolescence. Adolescence seldom manifests itself before the age of thirteen, so that the child of twelve is now classed with those who have begun to live another life. As has already been pointed out, there are deep seated physical and mental changes that take place between childhood and adolescence, so much so that we have now come to look upon the youth as having entered into an entirely different life. The importance then of separating the pupil until he has completed the full life of childhood is obvious. Youths and adults can be taught in the same class more successfully than children and adolescents. Moreover a teacher who thoroughly understands childhood is by no means competent to teach adolescents. The many futile attempts of the adult or child teacher to instruct adolescents may explain the great leakage of our Sunday-schools at this time of life. For this reason it is not only essential that children be kept separate from youth in the Sunday-school, but that teachers be specifically trained to deal with these distinct lives of the individual.

The matter of conversion also enters at this point. We shall have occasion to see in later study that the age of twelve is the logical year for this step. There are excellent reasons why decision for Christ should be the culmination of the instruction in the Junior department rather than the first objective of the Intermediate teacher.

In subsequent chapters the six periods here outlined will be taken up in order. We shall consider the physical, mental, social and spiritual characteristics of the child, as well as the required training that is essential for each period.

---

1. What are some of the factors that determine the age groups in our Sunday-schools?
2. What are the periods of child study and the corresponding departments of the Sunday-school?
3. What is the advantage in having three year periods for the Intermediate and Senior departments?
4. What disadvantage is there in this arrangement for the Junior department?
5. In what four divisions are the characteristics of each period considered?

Infancy

"Take this child."—Exodus 2:9.

IX

INFANCY

B Y THE time a child is seven he has received three-fourths of his education. Upon this foundation the subsequent physical, intellectual and spiritual structure will be built. Failure in the superstructure will naturally result when the foundation is not properly laid in the early and most impressionable years.

No higher tribute has ever been paid to early training than Paul's commendation of Timothy's instruction, "From a child thou hast known the scriptures, which are able to make thee wise unto salvation . . . Continue thou in the things which thou hast learned." Paul makes special mention of Timothy's grandmother Lois and his mother Eunice as being responsible for the unfeigned faith of his childhood. When the work of mother and grandmother and teacher has been well done in the early years of childhood, the instruction of subsequent teachers will be chiefly to "continue in the things which thou hast learned."

> "Early let us seek Thy favor,
> Early let us do Thy will;
> Blessed Lord and only Savior,
> With Thy love our bosoms fill."

All must recognize the potential possibilities that are wrapped up in every new born babe and the tremendous importance of making first impressions right impressions. Most of the perplexing questions that arise in childhood and adolescence can be answered by two words—*begin earlier*. For this reason, in the study and training of the child, we must commence at the very beginning.

1. Physically he is an actor.

His physical activities characterize him above everything else. He is seldom content to sit still and listen. He wants to go to things and handle them. Sometimes we are annoyed by his activity and call it restlessness. Man says, "Sit still." God says, "Wiggle." But there is a reason for all this activity. It fills a distinct purpose.

a. Activity is essential to growth.

The chief business of the infant is to grow, and with a continuous round of eating, sleeping and exercising he does grow. The first six months his weight doubles and in the first three years it increases four times. During the first year his height increases fifty per cent, and in the first three years seventy-five per cent. Nature has wisely provided that unless hindered the child will automatically take that exercise which is so essential to growth. For this reason not only should his activities be encouraged, but his arms and legs should be left free so that he can move easily.

b. Activity is essential to development.

We must be careful to distinguish between growth and development. Growth means simply increase in size. Development is a change in the character of the body tissues which makes for maturity and strength. There is a natural growth for all. Through physical activity, however, there comes the natural development that God intended. Along with the growth of the body there is the development of the senses. The child gradually pays attention to the impressions gained through touch, taste, smell, sight and hearing. This development is largely brought about through his activity.

c. Generated energy requires an outlet.

If you light a fire under a boiler and generate steam you store up energy. If no way of escape is provided for that steam, eventually the boiler will explode. Energy constantly generated naturally seeks a way of escape. This is also true of human energy, which finds its natural outlet in physical activity.

The child's program of continuous eating and sleeping is storing up energy which demands some avenue of escape. An adult can conserve his energy. He has learned to keep it in reserve and utilize it at times of special need, but a little child has no such control and the effort of his energy to find an outlet leads to his ceaseless activity.

d. The nervous system requires a response to impressions.

Impressions are constantly going to the brain over the sensory nerves and the answer that is returned over the motor nerves generally manifests itself through the muscles. In this very wonderful provision of nature, a response to every impression, lies the possibility of education. Bolton asserts, "The entire brain and nervous system suffer if motor activity is lacking during the growing period. The development of future mental powers lies in the improvement by the child of such opportunities as may be provided for the investigation of the senses and the testing of muscular control." We may understand the impression that a child receives from the corresponding expression that he gives. A mother comes to know what is troubling her child from this expression. He is not able to communicate to her his difficulty or the source of his unhappiness, but by tracing the expression back, the source of the impression may be discovered. In this way we have the index to the child's mind, truly a wonderful opportunity for study.

(1) Instincts impel actions.

Every child possesses natural tendencies which determine the character of his reaction to impressions. The instinct of curiosity manifests itself in the touching, taking and tearing actions of every baby. This instinct of curiosity so fundamental to education cannot be satisfied by reading or questioning. In *action alone* can the child acquire knowledge for himself. It has been demonstrated that natural instincts perish when repelled or neglected. Thus the good gifts of a gracious God may be lost from want of physical expression.

(2) Ideas impel actions.

Little children who have not acquired the reserve of adults generally say just what they think. The infant, as yet unable to talk, expresses his thoughts in action. His mind then may be read by his actions and this outward expression will determine the progress of his intelligence.

2. Mentally he is a discoverer.

The child at birth has no conscious intelligence. He has no knowledge. All that is most familiar to us is unknown to him. However, this condition swiftly changes as the months of the first year pass. Through his activities and discoveries he begins to have an understanding of things. His own activity in response to the variety of stimulation which he receives also furnishes him with further impressions and in similar manner these are interpreted.

As he grows through activity, he learns through discovery. Of course his discoveries are generally the result of his activities, so closely are the two related. Strangely enough, from this educative process of the infant we have one of the first laws of pedagogy. The great aim of the teacher, we are told, is to make the pupil a discoverer of truth. Deprived of the power of communication the babe sets out to discover for himself the new world into which he has come. He is a self-instructor, a self-teacher, and perhaps in this respect he is getting a more thorough education than his older brothers and sisters who have instructors. From the moment he opens his eyes to the light of the sun the child is making discoveries. First of all

a. He discovers his mother.

In the earliest hours she is all of heaven and earth to him. In his mother he has discovered protection, provision and Providence. The first object of a child's religion is its mother. The mother's arms are his heaven; her eyes, the stars; and her care and provision, the Providence on which he relies with fullness of faith.

b. He discovers his world.

It may be a very small world, limited to four walls which surround him, but it is nevertheless, in his estimation, a very large world. Into this world with eyes and ears and later with feet and hands, he sets out on voyages of discovery. He discovers that reaching, grasping, crying, brings him the things that he wants. As he has only a limited experience and as he acts without reflection, the problems that he can solve for himself are limited. Experience is his great teacher. For a while he bumps himself and tumbles around in his efforts to supply his great capacity for knowledge. But he soon grows in resourcefulness and in confidence. By experimentation he learns many things about natural laws and physical processes which years later may form a basis for generalization. In his discoveries he has the propensity for pulling things to pieces. But this is only that he may "cross the Atlantic" and see what is on the other side. He thoroughly enjoys feeling that he is doing something and making something happen.

c. He discovers himself.

The little child under three gradually grows to a consciousness of self as distinct from other members of the family. Ere long he recognizes himself in the mirror as a distinct personage. More than that he soon learns that he possesses a personality of his own. He finds there is a difference between "mine" and "yours." A baby is only a few weeks old when it begins to exercise its will upon its mother. In the occasional conflict of wills he is likely to discover that he does not always have to submit to the will of his mother unless he wishes to do so. A fond and foolish mother permits the child to have its own way because she dislikes to deny him what he wants. The child will fight against going to sleep at the proper time or contend for things which are injurious. He is pitting his will against the mother's, which means that he has discovered his personality. Parents need to guard against suppressing the personality on the one hand or developing a self-willed tyrant on the other. If the child is shy and retiring he needs to be encouraged in his efforts to promote his own interests. If he is extremely self-assertive it is important that he be taught to respect the wishes of others. This can be done without breaking his will.

3. Morally the child is an imitator.

Before the fourth year the child acquires his knowledge of right and wrong solely by imitation.

> a. *His religion will be a reflection of the religion he finds about him.*

We have already seen what a powerful influence the deep religious life of the Jewish mother had upon the children of that nation. The mother of the writer tells of an incident that happened in his life before he was old enough to talk. An older brother had been saying his evening prayer. Although the little fellow could not as yet express himself in language, he put up his little hands like his brother and tried to pray, beginning to cry because he could not speak.

There is no question but that the child in his earliest days is an imitator. "A father started for his office early one morning after a light fall of snow. Turning, he saw his two year old boy endeavoring to place his tiny feet in his own great footprints. The little fellow shouted, 'Go on. I'se comin', I'se comin', Papa, yite in ur tracks.' He caught the boy in his arms, carried him to his mother, then started again to his office. It had been his habit to stop on the way at a saloon for a glass of liquor. As he stood on the threshold that morning he seemed to hear a sweet voice calling, 'Go on, I'se comin', I'se comin', Papa, yite in ur tracks.' He stopped and looked the future squarely in the face and turned away."

If a mother in the presence of her child expresses some doubt about a statement of the holy Bible, he may become a habitual blasphemer when he is grown. If, on the other hand, she sits each evening by the bedside and teaches in the fading light of day, lessons of the

Saviour's love, the importance of truth, the virtue of kindness, industry, sympathy and sacrifice, some day that child may be a thundering Luther, a weeping Whitefield or a mighty Spurgeon.

> b. *His moral habits and attitudes will be largely determined by others.*

We speak of the "spoiled child," and that very phraseology ought to convince us that the child is not to blame. He has been spoiled by someone else. A child rocked to sleep by an indulgent mother may come to believe this is the proper method for the human race to seek repose. A fretful child can be soothed with a sugar pacifier and come to believe that the sweets, so ruinous to his physical and moral welfare, are the reward for his outbursts of ill temper.

The author knows of a child whose mother rebuked the good neighbor who came in to rock it. The little child had never been rocked in his life, nor was he permitted to have candy or sweets of any kind. At Christmas when one of the elders of the church brought candy to the home he could not understand why the mother would not allow the baby to eat it. As he grew older he never begged for pennies to buy candy, and today confectioneries may remain on the table without being a temptation. A child's bad habits are formed largely because of indulgent parents. Such habits become a part of us and the craving continues all through life.

> c. *Adult approval or disapproval of his first acts will be far reaching.*

If a mother cultivates a child's vanity, eulogizes his acts, calls out in his presence the admiration of spectators, pride and arrogance may rule his life. If, on the other hand, a mother praises a generous impulse, applauds an unselfish word, and rewards a kind act, we may later see a philanthropist. Parents should approve every act that promises physical, mental or moral development. To forbid a child to play with sand, or sweep the floor, and offer no substitute in allied activity, is to invite disobedience or to develop nervous affections. A parent should emphatically disapprove of every detrimental or disobedient act.

Miss Edna Baker tells the story of a baby of thirteen months who opened the door of the icebox repeatedly. "At first the mother shut the door quickly and spoke reprovingly to the child, later she carried him abruptly away from the vicinity of the icebox, finally she spatted his hands when caught in the act. After this last experience he would walk up to the box, put out his hand, then quickly withdraw it and scuttle away, making a wry face."

In discipline there is a golden medium between severity and laxity. The boy who is always beaten will be as bad as the boy who is never restrained. Love and patience are the powers in family government. John Wesley's mother told her husband that she admonished John twenty times because nineteen were not enough. She declared that her two boys were brought up on prayer and hickory. A rod is a confession of weakness, but we are all weak, and a wise mother will have a rod handy.

4. Training.

The Bible plainly declares that no teacher can take the place of the mother. God directed Pharaoh's daughter to the mother of Moses in those earliest hours when all the wealth and wisdom of the Egyptian court could not provide a better teacher. Both Joseph and

Daniel were exiled from home and country at an early age with nothing but a mother's training to sustain them amid the temptations and triumphs of pagan pomp and power.

But no mother has successfully brought up her children who has not first dedicated them to God. Many children have been failures in life because their selfish mothers had no wider vision of their usefulness beyond themselves. To be dedicated wholly does not mean to be given wholly to the mother. When young Matthew Simpson broke the news to his widowed mother that he felt called to preach, which would necessitate his leaving home, she exclaimed with tears of joy, "Oh, my son, I have prayed for this hour ever since you were born. At that time I dedicated you to the ministry." Campbell Morgan says, "My dedication to the ministry was maternal. Mother never told it to the baby, or the boy, but patiently waited."

Because there are fathers and mothers today without number who fail to recognize their children as a heritage from God and neglect to dedicate them to the Lord, the church provides

a. The Cradle Roll.

The Cradle Roll ministers to the needs of children from birth to their entrance into Sunday-school. Its purpose is threefold:

(1) To enroll a new scholar for the Sunday-school.

The Sunday-school gets a direct contact with the children through the Cradle Roll. In this way it shows an interest and a responsibility for the infants who come into the church family. The days go by and it is not long before these members of the Cradle Roll are ready to come into the Sunday-school.

Since we want to get a child from the very beginning it is very important that we start with the Cradle Roll. This not only insures the child being present when his religious education begins at the age of four, but it also indicates the interest of the church in his moral and spiritual welfare. With graded lessons it is not easy for us to admit scholars in later life any more than it is possible for our public schools to admit young men and young women who have not had any previous training. Therefore we should see that all of our boys and girls begin their religious education with the first of our graded lessons.

(2) To establish a point of contact between church and home.

I have never found a home so indifferent to the claims of religion that there have been objections to the babies being placed upon the Cradle Roll. The most godless parent is willing that the church should take this interest in his little child. A prayer offered up by a pastor in a home which has been blessed with a new-born child, is one that is not soon forgotten.

A young professional man told this simple story: "A while ago a baby came to my home. The little fellow seemed to be a gift from God and my heart was filled with a sacred reverence and tenderness which I did not have before. Your Cradle Roll visitors came down to my home and said they wanted the baby's name to put on the cradle roll of the church. They would pray for the boy every day and remember him in sickness and on his birthdays. Sometimes when I drive by your church I slow down a bit and say to myself, 'My baby's name is on the walls of that church somewhere and those people pray for him every day.' I had forgotten God and had wandered far from the church, but this little child has led me back.''

(3) To enlist parental training.

In many tactful ways the Cradle Roll superintendent or visitor is able to provide instruction to the parents. Many times a mother will welcome a prayer suggested by the church visitor, or any other instruction that may be helpful. This is very important when we realize how much the child learns in the first two years before he comes to the church.

b.   Cradle Roll class.

Because of the failure of parents in such large numbers to provide religious education in the home, the Cradle Roll class has been instituted for the three-year-old child. This class should be kept separate from the Beginners' department in order not to jeopardize the more important work of the older children. If it is not possible to have a separate room for this group, it would not be wise to attempt to classify them with the Beginners. As the average number of this age in a Sunday-school of one hundred is only four, the group at best will be small. To meet the needs of these very little children the use of object lessons is recommended.

---

1. Why must religious education begin in infancy?
2. Give four reasons for an infant's activity.
3. What should be our attitude toward this activity?
4. What three discoveries does the infant make?
5. Show how a child reflects the religion he finds about him.
6. How are moral habits and attitudes determined?
7. What should be the attitude of the adult to the first acts of the infant?
8. How should discipline be exercised?
9. In what way does a child's dedication affect his future?
10. What is the threefold purpose of the Cradle Roll?

"Suffer the little children to come unto me."—Mark 10:14.

X

EARLY CHILDHOOD

THE passing of the child from infancy to early childhood is so gradual that few would be able to mark a change at any given time. As his body lengthens his field widens and his mind deepens. He carries over many of the characteristics of infancy but they assume a new relationship and therefore are known by a different name. His environment is enlarged to include the Sunday-school, kindergarten and playground, so that teachers and playmates are now forces to be recognized as having a place in the making of his life.

1. Physically he is a player.

The activity that so conspicuously marked his infancy now manifests itself in play. The little child is a player and all his world a playground. Eating, sleeping and playing is the threefold program of his daily existence. To be sure he carries his play on into later life, but because in these early years other interests have not as yet interrupted his life of play, we can well consider it at this point. To his elders play time may appear to be lost time, but such is not the case. Play has great values for body, mind and character. While, like activity, play is generally associated with the physical side, it is also a very important factor in the mental, social and moral development.

a. *Play is a physical trainer.*

Between the ages of four and seven there is a great enlargement of the limbs. This explains why running constitutes the important part of the games of this period. The large muscles of the trunk, limbs and arms develop so rapidly that there is an increase of forty-five per cent in weight. To further this development the child is almost ceaselessly in motion. Nature spurs him on so that his movements are not all under control. O'Shea calls our attention to the fact that when lively children are forced to sit still, automatic movements of the head, hands and feet are still in evidence. The result of such enforced quiet is disastrous. On the other hand, the endurance of children is slight and they tire quickly of either mental or muscular effort. For this reason games should not be prolonged and periods of study should be made as brief as possible. Change is the keyword to the child's program. All the physical value that work brings to an adult, play provides for a child.

b. *Play is a mental instructor.*

The mind of a child is never so clearly revealed as in play. He is at home in his own world with no thought of conforming to the rules and restrictions of others.

(1) *Childish instincts expressed in play.*

These instincts work out through the senses and so the sense perceptions are developed. "If you watch a young child play," says Taylor, "you are amused by the number, variety and vigor of his movements. Many of these give good exercise but are a complete waste of energy so far as the result of the game is concerned. Gradually as he plays more he learns to suppress these, to utilize and to concentrate energy. This is one of the earliest and best lessons in self-control."

(2) Childish imaginations expressed in play.

The child thinks largely in mental pictures. He develops these photographs by play and they become real to him. Hall declares that for a number of years the imagination is the chief means of training and that the child should not only have material to stimulate his imagination but opportunity to express it in play. There is nothing like story telling to launch a child into his world of make-believe, and in his play we find he makes no clear distinction between imagination and reality. "The unimaginative child," Forbush tells us, "is usually the child who has not played widely." Having had but limited experiences he goes forth into the real world with timidity. It is the play that reproduces the child's imagination and gives him the self-confidence of experience to take the initiative in later life. Poets, artists, inventors were once children of strong imaginations.

Imaginative fears can be easily created at this time and it is possible to make a child a coward for life by frightening the little one with threats of goblins and witches. The disobedient boy or girl is sometimes threatened with the police or the bogey-man. Those who deal with a child at this imaginative age must be particularly careful not to terrify him by accounts of things which will frighten and alarm him.

(3) Childish imitations expressed in play.

Children's games are mostly imitations of some experience that has impressed them. Jeffs tells a story of two children, four and six, respectively, who caught scarlet fever and were sent to the quarantine hospital. When they returned home the favorite game for weeks was hospital. All available dolls were laid on the sofa, which was the ward. The girl was nurse. The boy went in, sometimes grave, sometimes cheery, with the inquiry, "Well, nurse, how are the patients? I will take their temperature." He took it and gave an opinion as to the state of each patient.

The values of imaginative play are many. It stimulates childish thinking. He remembers best what he learns in this way. He understands actions, purposes, traits and customs through his mimicry, his life being enlarged when he puts himself in the place of another.

How the propensity of a child to imitate a person he admires may be utilized by the parent to gain a purpose, is illustrated by Alma Sheridan:

"It is John's bedtime, but mother sees that John is not in a very good humor for going to bed and that an effort to make him go will result in a struggle. So she says cheerfully, 'Come now, Policeman John, it is time to go off duty and have a sleep.' John pauses a moment. He knows that he doesn't want to go to bed. Still he does so much want to be a policeman, so off he goes." It will not do to try to impose an ideal which the child does not admire. If John did not care about being a policeman the game would not have been successful.

c. *Play is a social equalizer.*

The companions of infancy are closely confined to the home circle, but the child now adds many outsiders to his widening acquaintance. The child of three likes to be with other children, but when he has reached the age of four or five he wants to engage in their games. At first the self-assertiveness he has acquired through his individual rule in the nursery manifests itself in a desire to play all the parts, but soon he is willing that others should have a place in the game. These games not only check the growing spirit of egotism in their leveling process, but teach him the importance of teamwork. A little fellow was pulling in a family tug-o'-war during the Christmas holidays. He took his place at the end, put his arms as far as they would go around an aunt and when his side pulled the other side over he cried, "We won, I pulled."

   d. Play is a moral teacher.

Public opinion, as expressed in the attitude of playmates is a respected teacher. The child who sulks if he cannot have his own way is soon taught by the consensus of his companions that selfishness and stubbornness mean self-exile. The penalty of ostracism decreed by this juvenile court is an effective school for the spoiled child. Tantrums and tears may avail with a foolish, fond mother, but they are ruled out by the court of public opinion.

A child's sense of honor and justice is revealed in play. The boy or girl who seeks to gain the advantage by some underhanded means is never popular. A boy or girl may have done wrong, but those who know of it and do not approve of it will suffer punishment themselves rather than reveal the person. Children have their own laws and they have their own ways of meting out justice. Among the ways is that of not telling upon others. They are not so sure that the justice of the elders is always as even-handed as it is stern.

2. Mentally he is a questioner.

The last but by no means the least discovery of the infant is that he has an individuality and will of his own. The discovery of his enlarged world and his own

personal relationship to this unfolding life, leads him
to ask his never-ending questions. As an infant he
solved his problems by his activities and by his adven-
tures of discovery, but now that he can talk, the question
is the first and foremost method of obtaining information.
Those who have read "Sweet Cicely" remember the boy
and his propensity to ask questions. He might have been
called "Say," because "Say" was always on his lips.
George Perin in a charming little story entitled, "Why,
Fadder? Why?" has chronicled some of the questions
that a talkative little son asked on an auto ride:

"Fadder, what makes de auto go?
  Why does a wagon have horses?
  Do de horses make de wagon go?
  How does de bird fly?
  Who made de birds' wings?
  Does de cloud fly like de bird?
  Does de cloud have wings too?
  Fadder, if de cloud has dot no wings, den how does it fly?
  Why do de birds build their nests in de trees?
  What makes de wain fall down?
  How does de wain get up in de clouds?
  What makes de flowers grow?
  Who puts de color in de flowers?
  Fadder, what makes us be living?"

Parents and teachers realize that it takes a great deal
of patience to answer the run of questions that proceed
from a little child. Only too often his inquiries are
suppressed. Children are told that speech is silver and
silence is golden, that they should be seen and not heard,
but in view of all that is involved it is questionable
whether any child should be taken out where he is sure
to make new discoveries only to be deprived of the right
of being heard. In silencing speech there is a grave
danger that we may suppress a natural quest for knowledge as well as a natural quest for expression. It is
well for us to note that

a. *Encouragement or discouragement of a child's questions will affect his education.*

In pedagogy we learn that the educational process begins only when the pupil asks questions. The child's question then is the index to his mind. The question reveals the fact that he is mentally present and his understanding is prepared for the answer. But if parent or teacher persists in telling him something in which he is not interested, or questions him about things beyond his understanding, *ignoring his questions,* there is little value to the instruction.

b. *Encouragement or discouragement of a child's questions will affect his personality.*

The child's question is not only an index to his mind, but the index to himself. The question is a manifestation of self-realization and self-seeking. This is not selfishness but simply nature. Self-assertion and self-denial are only possible when self-realization exists in its fullest extent. This is the time for the development of the personality. To wholly repress efforts of self-assertiveness will cause the child to become weak-willed and incapable of taking the initiative. Because of this fact all questions should be recognized and judiciously answered, that the child may have wisdom rather than knowledge and confidence rather than conceit. Frequently I am interrupted during family prayers by my little boy's questions. Is it right for me to allow this period to be invaded by such untimely interruptions? It may seem out of place to older people, but these questions represent the very life of the child. He is thinking about God and about God's Word. Moreover he is thinking about it in terms of his own life. Is it not right then to encourage such questions? Many a

Sunday-school teacher of older boys and girls has found them slow to ask questions simply because their first interrogations were reproved and repressed. Many a Sunday-school teacher has waited in vain to hear from the lips of the older child that all-important question, "What must I do to be saved?" And the question has never been asked because self was repressed earlier in life and there has never been enough of self to realize a personal relationship to Jesus Christ and assert its claim upon His atonement.

While we want to give the personality every opportunity to develop, we need to guard against the making of a self-willed tyrant. Self-realization does not require self-admiration, and self-assertion need never pass beyond parental control. The active, energetic child who is more impulsive than reflective, needs to be taught truths which will tend to make him think before acting. He may need to be reminded that there is a time for questions, a time for answers and a time for children.

3. Religiously he is a believer.

Perhaps it was just such a child that Christ took up in His arms and said, "Whosoever shall not receive the kingdom of God as a little child, he shall not enter therein." "Faith, without which it is impossible to please God," is predominant in a child of four to five. The little child believes everything you tell him, simply because of his lack of experience. What you tell him about wolves and bears, tramps and robbers, giants and goblins, angels and devils, grows appallingly in that vivid ideal world in which he lives. If his parents have always been truthful and he has come to know that they mean what they say, he will believe them implicitly. Many letters and prayers every year witness how real is Santa Claus to the little child, as well as the bogey-man and other fanciful creations that some indiscreet parent has revealed to him. If a mother tells a child some bugaboo will come and catch him because he is bad, the fear excited may make the child a coward, and the fact that he finds out there is no bugaboo, may make him a liar. Whether a child develops a keen appreciation of the truth or becomes a deceiver will depend largely upon his surroundings.

Parents and teachers should be absolutely truthful in answering the child's questions. If the reply is honest it should satisfy while the explanation need not be beyond the child's power of comprehension. A child asked his father this difficult question, "Father, who made God?" "No one made God, my boy, He always was." The child was puzzled for a moment and then he said slowly, "I don't think I can understand that." "Neither do I understand it, my boy," said the father frankly, "there are some things that puzzle the wisest men." This father showed a great deal of wisdom and honesty in the answer he gave to the difficult question of his boy. A child will often find his own answer if your reply fails to satisfy, but he will respect you the more for a confession of limitation in knowledge in such cases.

Even when every effort is made to surround the child with truth it is possible and not improbable that he will discover a lie even in this early period. Forbush says, "Most of the lying of little children is due to fancy. What they heard out of a book yesterday or dreamed in the night gets mixed up with what they saw today and is reported with faulty memory."

A child's prevarications may be divided into three classes:

a. Exaggerated statements.

Possibly he may have overheard his parents speak in superlative terms so frequently that he has formed the habit. It may be he desires to make a great impression and so he tells big stories about himself. The tendency to exaggerate is always natural in a home where the conversation is extravagant.

b. Inaccurate replies.

These are partly due to inattention and partly to forgetfulness. He is not able to answer accurately and so he gives the easiest answer that occurs to him.

c. Profitable deception.

Children do not usually form the habit of deliberate and wilful lying unless they find it profitable to do so. A child may discover a lie to be a very present help in time of trouble, and acquire the habit of lying when he finds that his act is not discovered or that punishment follows if he confesses. For this reason a lie should never pass unnoticed or unconfessed. A fond mother may be horrified to find a lie upon the lips of her little boy, but any failure upon her part to recognize and rectify it will more fully establish the evil in the child's life. On the other hand, the administration of punishment may only lead to further deception. It is all important that we keep the lines of communication open between the child and the parent. A child should be encouraged to tell everything and conceal nothing from father and mother. The best policy to pursue is to teach the child the horrors of a lie and the happiness of repentance and restoration. A ten-year old boy added a new interpretation to the Washington cherry tree story when he said, ''It was no trouble to tell the truth when one had such a kind father." A truth telling child depends, to a large extent, upon truth loving parents.

4. Training.

Training of the little child is divided between home, kindergarten and Sunday-school. The mother still remains the greatest of all teachers and as yet she cannot afford to relinquish her place to others. Greater progress can often be made with a diligent mother, especially where schools are poorly organized and the teachers are not trained for their work. The mother of the writer made it her purpose to spend Sunday afternoon with her two boys even after they had passed the years of early childhood. A very insistent pastor was anxious that she should teach in the Sunday-school. He said that the children would be well cared for in the Infant department. The mother therefore put her two boys in that department in order that she might have the opportunity to teach in the Sunday-school. The first Sunday when they came home they began to tussle with one another and behave in extraordinary manner. After this had gone on for several Sundays she resolved to go and visit that Infant department. She found it utterly lacking in discipline and order and decided it was far better that she stay home and teach her boys than submit them to such an environment.

It is necessary that our Beginner's department be conducted with order and care if we are to gain the respect of the parents who entrust their little ones to us. We need organized administration, graded lessons, and trained teachers for the Beginner's department as for any other department.

Home and school should further a threefold program of

a. Worship.

As a child comes to love his father and mother he may likewise come to love God. His worship will be the expression of his feelings toward the God with whom he has become acquainted by the worship of his parents. The child, however, cannot understand God as Creator or Sovereign, but only as a Father. Gratitude will probably be the underlying cause of his love and reverence and its expression will be found in praise, prayer and offering.

(1) Praise.

If it is to be the child's praise we would not teach a hymn that is applicable for later experience or that can be comprehended only by adults.

> "In the sky above,
> Where the angels dwell,
> God doth ever love us,
> We should love Him well."

> "Do you know how many stars
> There are shining in the sky,
> Do you know how many clouds
> Every day go sailing by?
> God in heaven hath counted all
> He would miss one should it fall."

> "Can a little child like me
> Thank the Father fittingly?
> Yes, oh, yes, be good and true,
> Patient, kind in all you do."

(2) Prayer.

A child's prayers should express his own feelings as much as his praise. The juvenile evening prayer based upon Psalm 4:8 is familiar to most children:

> "Now I lay me down to sleep
> I pray thee, Lord, my soul to keep."

Just as fitting for morning devotion is

"Father, we thank Thee for the night,
And for the pleasant morning light,
For rest and food and loving care,
And all that makes the day so fair."

As soon as the child becomes familiar with the set prayers he has been taught, he may be encouraged to add expressions of personal gratitude or petitions for some childish need as his enlarged experiences may suggest. Sometimes after asking God's blessing upon father and mother, the child will think of the domestic servant, the cat or the dog, or the wooden horse. Sometimes there will be petitions for something that is on the heart of the little one. These tendencies to individualize his prayer should not be suppressed for it is only a manifestation of his unquestioned faith in the power and goodness of God. God in heaven is often very near to the life of a little child.

(3) Giving.

Giving is a very important form of worship, and the foundation for generous habits in later life may be successfully laid at this time. The lessons may be lost, however, if parents provide the children pennies for the Sunday-school and larger amounts for candy and other things. You may remember the story of the penny and the dollar that had a controversy as to which was the more religious. "Upon me," said the dollar, "is stamped the inscription, 'In God We Trust,' while there is nothing to designate you but the head of a heathen." "Oh, I don't know," said the penny, "I go to church every Sunday." The financial problem of the church to make every member a liberal contributor can be solved by an educational program of systematic, sympathetic giving that will be put into operation during the earliest years of childhood.

(2) Nature lessons.

b. Instruction.

The Bible contains moral and religious truth better adapted to the needs of the individual from infancy to old age than can be found in any other book. It is not difficult to see, however, that the truths of the Bible written for adults are neither interesting nor educational for a little child. Mathematics has a wide application, from the multiplication table in the early grades to the logarithms of civil engineering. We would not attempt to teach children trigonometry until they had first mastered the multiplication table. In like manner our diet is adapted to all ages. There is milk for babies and meat for adults. Paul used this illustration in the use of the Bible: "Ye have need of milk, and not of strong meat. For everyone that useth milk is unskillful in the word of righteousness: for he is a babe. But strong meat belongeth to them that are of full age, even those who by reason of use have their senses exercised to discern both good and evil." We have both example and authority for grading our biblical material and nothing but the graded lessons should ever be used in the Beginner's department. These will provide instruction about

(1) God as a Heavenly Father.

If God is pictured to the child as the loving Heavenly Father who cares for him just as his own father with whom he is familiar, provides food to eat and water to drink and clothing to wear, the Heavenly Father who made the beautiful world and all the things in it; the heart of the little child will go out in love and trust to Him.

To deprive a little child of lessons from nature, is to

rob him of one of his most precious spiritual inheritances, one of the ways in which God most clearly speaks to his soul. Our lessons should take account of the seasons, providing work appropriate to spring, summer, autumn and winter. There is a religion of nature to the child. He sees the world as God's world. And the world is a beautiful world and suggests beautiful thoughts of God. God makes the harvest grow and clothes the earth with grass and flowers, as surely as mother provides the dinner and father brings candy and toys. Jesus always viewed the world as the work of the Father and referred to the lilies of the field, the growing grain, the trees, the handiwork of God, who is very near to us and whose joy is to see His children happy in a world made for a happy family.

(3) Child lessons.

The interest of a little child in other children assures beyond question that the Bible stories of children are the first ones we should teach them.

c. Discipline.

Discipline is the duty of the home, particularly in the enforcement of the fifth commandment. One of our leading newspapers recently made this comment: "If we had more old-fashioned spanking in Chicago there would be an impressive lesson that the hand of the parent in childhood often obviates the hand of the law in later life." The newer education, in its very proper emphasis upon self-expression, is in danger of going beyond the bounds of parental control. Parents may permit self to run riot, and forget that the greatness of a personality is not self-assertion but self-control and that restraint is the principal function of reason. Parents must encourage expression and at the same time exercise discipline. Parents stand in the place of God to their children in a great many ways until the children arrive at the age of discretion. If children are true to their parents it will be easy for them to be true to God. God exalts human relationship as symbolic of our relation to Him by both law and grace. God is our Father in heaven. We are the offspring. We can never understand the love and care of God until we have learned how dear and loving are our father and mother. We can never understand the honor and reverence due God until we have learned how much we owe to our parents. Children can never obey the Heavenly Father as they should until they have first learned to obey earthly parents. Obedience and respect toward parents prepare the way for obedience due the employer, and joined with other virtues, they help toward a prosperous career and honored old age. Disobedience and disrespect for parents are generally the first stages in a downward career. A boy and girl who cannot obey their parents will never be able to obey the laws of the land. Hence not only the preservation of the home but also the safety of the nation lies in the enforcement of the Fifth Commandment.

———————

1. What is the difference between the environment of an infant and a little child?
2. What are the four values of play?
3. Why should a program for little children be frequently changed?
4. In what three ways is play a mental instructor?
5. Why should a child's imagination be encouraged?
6. Why are childish imitations of educative value?
7. How does the play of children tend to check the spirit of egotism in the individual?
8. How does play tend to correct selfishness and dishonesty?
9. What has a child's questions to do with his education?
10. What has a child's questions to do with his personality?

11. What has the encouragement of a child's questions to do with his own conversion?

12. When should questions be suppressed?

13. What can you say of the faith of a little child?

14. How should we deal with a child's religious questions?

15. Name three ways in which falsehoods begin.

16. How should we deal with deliberate deceptions?

17. Why does a good home afford better training than a disorderly Beginner's department?

18. What is the threefold program of training for the little child?

19. What hymns are suitable for this age?

20. Why should children be encouraged to individualize their prayer?

21. How may the foundation for generous habits be laid in childhood?

22. What reasons can you give for the use of graded lessons in the Beginner's department?

23. What three lines of instruction will a graded program provide?

24. Give several reasons why the Fifth Commandment should be enforced at this time.

Middle Childhood

"Train up a child in the way he should go."—Proverbs 22:6.

XI

MIDDLE CHILDHOOD

PSYCHOLOGISTS agree that there is no marked transition between early and middle childhood. Rather this span of years from six to eight constitutes a transition period in itself, since it marks the passing of the child from home to school, play to work, instinct to will, and imagination to reason. The fact that the child now enters school gives him a wider experience and provides him a distinct place in the social order. His circle of companionship is enlarged and a more definite round of responsibility is assumed.

1. Physically he is a hustler.

In contrast with the former period which is spoken of as sensory, this is often called the motor period. The child is more violently active and energetic and to sit still for any length of time is torture. This restless nature which leads to ceaseless activity serves an important purpose in furthering growth and development. There is a rapid growth of no less than thirty-one per cent but far more important than the enlargement of the body is its development. There is a control of the senses and muscular action that afford greater perception and accuracy of movement. This drilling of his muscles in walking, running, climbing, throwing, tends to render these movements automatic. Such fundamental, physical habits once perfected, the mind is liberated for other purposes. Thus the mental growth may be advanced or retarded in so far as muscular control or co-ordination progresses.

It is evident that there is a greater need than ever for a large program of activity. Much of his time will be spent in

a. Play.

There are several distinctions to consider in comparing the play life of early and middle childhood.

(1) He no longer plays alone.

His entrance to school provides him with companions. Play is no longer individualistic but takes the form of games with very simple rules. Heretofore, all play centered in himself, but now there is a growing willingness to co-operate with others and to promote the interests of the group rather than those of the individual. Play takes the form of games in which rivalry and competition begin. This has a tendency to speed up his activities and it is quite possible for him to exhaust his strength. His supply of reserve vitality is limited and he is easily fatigued with any strenuous or prolonged exercise. The play program should provide frequent rest periods to prevent physical exhaustion.

(2) His play is more purposeful.

It is no longer the aimless exercise of former days but there is evidence of purposeful construction. He desires to attain skill in certain movements, like throwing the ball, so that he may have a place in the game. He wants to make things and achieve something. Toys mean much more to him now than formerly. And the more he can do with them the greater will be his enjoyment. The mechanical toy that is wound up and does only one thing soon loses its interest. On the other hand, a pile of blocks which will lend themselves to a variety of ar-

rangement will prove more pleasing and practical.
Simple home-made toys that can be adapted to the constructive instincts of the child are far better than play
things that merely amuse. It is the joy in activity that
is the essence of play rather than passive admiration
of a mechanical perfection. Something to do and something to make should be the objective in all plans for
his play.

(3) Play and playmates will be determined by sex.

Already at five or six we may note some difference
between boys and girls in their choice of pursuits. Boys
find more interest in vigorous games that require scrimmages and scrambles. Girls find more enjoyment with
their dolls and all the miniature furniture that will be
required by a little housekeeper. The undressed doll
will call for a seamstress and a milliner, but the boy's
handwork is more likely to be in the direction of making kites, boats, tops and crude toys.

b. Work.

Many attempts have been made to differentiate work
from play but without success. It is evident that they
have a common origin and in this early period of life
there is little distinction. As one small boy said, "Work
is play you don't like and play is work you do like."
The child instinctively plays at what is later to be his
work. He may and at times does employ his activities
voluntarily in work as well as in play. Where the
imagination has been properly trained he passes from
play to work without experiencing the drudgery with
which work is associated in later life. On this account
the foundation for habits of industry can be easily laid
at this time. Aside from filling a distinct need in promoting physical development, work has

(1) Educative value.

Dr. Walker and Prof. Hall have demonstrated the far-reaching results in educational development that are possible when children are apprenticed to their parents in farm and household tasks. Babson, the statistician, says that the reason the great industrial leaders come from the country rather than the city is because the boy on the farm has been trained to work. The greatest educator of the previous generation was not the public school but the woodbox. There is a distinct advantage for every child who has a woodbox to fill or chores to do about the home. By nature a boy likes to produce. Give him a knife and let him whittle out a top and some day he may be a carpenter. The girl who uses her scissors to cut out a dress for her doll is only getting ready to cut out her own dresses and do her own sewing. The child that has learned at home to work steadily, carefully and yet quickly will be a great asset to industry. The fact that he acquires a habit of doing work in this way eliminates waste and greatly increases his efficiency.

(2) Social value.

Work affords more social contacts than play. It provides the companionship of older children and adults that play seldom permits. Parents who find it difficult to fill a place in the play of their child obtain fellowship in work. As a "helper" to the parent, not only is the child in a position to appreciate the importance of co-operation, but to acquire such principles as application, concentration and perseverance, if they are inherent in his parents. In co-operative work a parent is able to impart knowledge far better than by instruction. A child can learn how to do something much sooner through having it performed before his eyes than from verbal directions. Moreover he will never learn to rely upon himself unless he has been a partaker of home duties that require industry, patience and resourcefulness. A sense of partnership in promoting the interests of the home is a natural result of participation in its tasks. Boys and girls come to feel that they have a distinct place and a distinct part in the home because they contribute their share in doing the work.

(3) Moral value.

The Bible very plainly points out the close relationship between work and character. As someone has said, "The Devil tempts other men, but idle men tempt the Devil." Idleness is the parent of crime as industry is the father of contentment. "God gave us work," says Henry Drummond, "not so much that the world needs it, but because the worker needs it. Men make work but work makes men." A factory or a farm is not merely a place for making money but a place for making men. God's greatest concern is the making of men and it is work, not money, that makes men. The lack of having something practical and profitable to do in these days of increasing idleness is proving most disastrous to youth. A dread of hard work sends more adolescents into crime than poverty or ignorance. The fact that more than one-half of our population now live in cities and for the most part in rented apartments, has robbed the children of the birthright of industry and substituted the pottage of joy rides and moving picture shows. The only safeguard for adolescents in this atmosphere of "pride, fullness of bread, and abundance of idleness" is to multiply his interests in things worth while. Whether he becomes interested in industrious pursuits, however, will largely depend upon the habits of work he has acquired in childhood. No one dreads hard labor who is accustomed to work. Parents cannot deprive their children of training in work and confidently expect them to suddenly acquire industrious inclinations in later life. Invariably the character of adolescence is built upon the habits of childhood.

The far-reaching value of a program of work in the home is well illustrated from the reminiscences of United States Senator Ferris, of Michigan: "When I was a boy, on one occasion I asked my father for a top. He said, 'Make it. Mother will give you a spool and here is my pocket knife.'

"I whittled for a few minutes and found the cutting difficult. I returned the knife to father and he said, 'Where is the top?'

"I said, 'I don't want a top.'

"He replied, 'You do want a top. Make it or I'll be obliged to punish you.'

"I was so well acquainted with my father that I made the top. When I returned his knife he commended me by spinning it and remarking, 'That's a fine top.'

"My father builded better than he knew. He put lime in my spine and thought in my brain by insisting that I make my own tops, wagons, sleds, kites, boats, and that I complete every task I voluntarily began. Modern fathers and mothers have forgotten the fine art of demanding that the boys help themselves. The toy shop, through thoughtless fathers and mothers, has dissipated the energies of our boys and placed a premium on helplessness. My father never gave me a nickel in his life. He gave me many opportunities to earn nickels. Father never borrowed any of my money and forgot to pay it back. If I made a bad investment he told me not to whine but to learn through experience. Because of this training I never saw a day in my life when I could not get some kind of useful work to do. On the one hundred acre home in southern New York I was thoroughly and adequately educated for the struggles of life. Through the untiring efforts of my father and mother I learned the fine arts of industry, self-sacrifice, self-reliance, honesty, sobriety, economy and abiding loyalty to my parents. My home training has been the key to my success. Father and mother were my great teachers.''

2. Mentally he is an observer.

Perception is quicker, more acute and more definite than in the previous stage. The child observes more closely now as a result of his greater knowledge, but even more so because of the acuteness of his senses. He revels in the feel of the wind and the rain and the snow. He loves to splash in the water, wade through the snow and paddle in the mud. He delights in the noises that formerly frightened him. The instinct of curiosity urges him to examine and explore. There is also an increased power of attention and a greater faculty of observation. Sight and hearing are very acute and frequently he will note things long before they attract the attention of an adult.

But while a child now has eyes to see and ears to hear the things that escape the notice of the mentally absorbed adult, he is far from understanding these new sights and scenes. The powers of reasoning and discrimination are only just awakening and we may easily overestimate a child's intellectual progress at this time. The investigations of Professor Hall reveal the fact that sixty per cent of the children entering school do not know a robin, ninety per cent could not distinguish an elm tree, while seventy per cent could not locate their wrists and twenty-five per cent, their elbows. The mental understanding does not keep pace with the increased power of observation because the child in his growing world is constantly meeting with experiences that are entirely new to him. His mental progress depends largely upon

a. The law of apperception.

Apperception is that mental process through which new conceptions are interpreted in terms of the old. It is the sum total of the understanding. The law of apperception is the interpretation of each new experience by its relation to one's ideas, instincts and habits. This law of association or contact is fundamental to all child training. The new can only be understood in terms of the old.

A little child had lived all her life in Florida until one winter, she went North. Upon looking out of the window she saw what appeared to be "white feathers" falling from the sky. That was her conception of snow. If children tell you that chickens come from crates, apples from boxes, milk from bottles, you know at once that they live in the city with no experience of the country and things of nature. If they believe that butterflies make butter, that ants are some kind of aunts, you may realize that language has led them astray. Bible expressions sometimes are given such interpretation through association of sounds and ideas, "That wicked flea when no man pursueth," "I would rather be a door key in the house of the Lord."

Our Lord was a master of the law of apperception. His hearers were all familiar with the Old Testament. For this reason He constantly built new truth upon these well known facts. His crucifixion upon the cross was to be similar to the lifting up of the brazen serpent in the wilderness. His burial and resurrection were to be likened to the experiences through which Jonah had passed. The times of His return would be like the days of Noah and the days of Lot. He described things that were to come in terms of things that had already happened.

To understand what the pupil's experience has been, what ideas and habits he has acquired, is the primary duty of every teacher. Before attempting to impart new information the teacher should undertake to explore carefully, section by section, the children's minds with all the tact and ingenuity she can command and seek to determine exactly what is already known. The parents, who understand better than anyone else the environment and instruction to which their child has been subjected, are best able to explain the new impressions his observations produce. A close relationship between parent and teacher will be of great value to the latter in unfolding the mind of the child. Someone has said that if every mother could be a teacher and every teacher a mother, we should have in the happy combination educators of greater understanding.

The Sunday-school teacher may likewise gain a practical entrance into the child's perceptions by visiting his grade at school and familiarizing herself with his studies and surroundings. The home contact and the school contact during the week are the teacher's best aids in making the religious contact on Sunday.

b. Physical efficiency.

Many children have limited powers of observation because of physical deficiency. It was the war which first

awakened us to a realization of our shortcomings as a
nation from the standpoint of physical effectiveness.
More than forty per cent of the drafted men showed
physical shortcomings, many of which would be a serious
handicap in their intellectual progress.   Often a child
falls behind in school not because he is mentally deficient
but because he is physically impaired.   If these defects
can be recognized and rectified as the child enters school
it will enable him to have an equal chance with other
boys and girls.   The most common defect appears in
the form of decayed teeth.   Eighty per cent of the
American children have dental defects which more or
less impair the general health.   Defective vision affects
from fifteen to thirty per cent of all children to a serious
degree, and abnormal tonsils and adenoids will appear
in ten to twenty per cent of any average group.   Defective hearing is the least common, but its peculiar
importance to school work makes any impairment a
serious handicap.   We owe it to our children to see that
they have a fair opportunity in life by rectifying any
physical deficiency that they may have.

3.   Religiously he is a discriminator.

The child is naturally God-inclined.   His conscience
is tender, the impulse to obey is strong and the implicit
faith of the earlier years still lingers with him.   But
while the child is very credulous, he now begins to prepare himself for investigation in later life, for proof and
certainty.   He seeks proof first by the use of the senses
and muscles.   Next he appeals to authority.   He uses
such expressions as "Honest truly," "Honor bright,"
"Hope to die," "Cross my heart," to test the veracity
of your testimony.   He has a spiritual hunger for real

things which asserts itself in the critical attitude he exhibits. He discriminates between

a. Fact and fiction.

The story has just as much charm as in earlier years, but the invariable question, "Is it really true?" is sure to follow its conclusion with almost painful eagerness. Life is becoming very real to him and he requires real things to satisfy his longings. Somewhere about the age of six the Santa Claus myth is discovered. From the absence of chimneys, reindeer and other essential accessories, his faith in a heretofore accepted fact is shattered. It is important that the parent truthfully explain this mythological character at the first symptom of incredulity. To neglect this explanation with the hopes of continued deception will prove disastrous. The child will believe his mother and father until the truth has been forced upon him by the ridicule of his playmates. He has been deceived by his parents and left to find out most ignominiously the truth from another. Yet he ought to have a desire to come to his parents before anyone else in the world for the truth and with the truth.

With the Santa Claus myth there will also be the stork delusion that will likewise have to be explained. There are no visible storks, but there are on the other hand plain facts that sooner or later will puzzle every child. He may not be ready to receive the whole truth on this subject but all answers should be honest. The parent who deceives or denies his boy is only dismissing him to secure the facts of life from impure and unholy sources.

The Bible must be presented now as it will be taught in later years. The reason that so many adolescents have had their religious faith shattered is because their teachers have designated as fiction what they were taught as facts during the most impressionable years of their life. They have not only lost faith in the Bible and in God, but confidence in home and in church, where they have always come to look for the truth and nothing but the truth.

No wonder the little girl was puzzled when her teacher cast doubt upon the veracity of a Bible story which had always seemed real to her. Her question illustrates the attitude of mind in every little child whose believing nature is rudely shocked for the first time, "Well, if God didn't mean what He said, why didn't He say what He meant?"

The only way to save a child from the *agony* of doubt is to begin with the truth and stick to it. Not that it is necessary for parent and teacher to explain every passage of Scripture—even a child will ask questions that even the wisest of men cannot answer. It is sufficient to say that "God who cannot lie," hath spoken, and in order that His children may exercise their faith He does not always reveal everything to them. The parental relationship can be used again and again to solve the child's theological problems.

Miss Mumford tells of a boy who said one night to his father after some quiet thought, "Father, I don't understand why I can't hear God when he speaks just as I hear you. Samuel did. It says so in the Bible. But I have tried for ever so long and I can't hear anything."

The father wanting to help the boy looked lovingly at him, and the child, feeling his tenderness, ran and nestled in his arms. The father asked why he came and the boy said, "Because I knew that you wanted me."

Then the way was open to explain to the child that in the same way when we know and love God, the Heavenly Father, we feel His love and His thoughts without hearing any audible voice.

b. Right and wrong.

The child now begins to understand something of the great conflict that is going on in this world between the forces of good and evil. He recognizes that he himself is being drawn into the warfare. There is beginning to come to him the universal experience of moral failure and a realization of his own weakness. He discovers that there are good boys and bad boys whose associations are likely to affect his own character. He discriminates between right and wrong acts on his part, not only by the consequences but by the effect on his own peace and happiness. A lie at eight is a far more serious matter than a falsehood at four. Conscience enters in to trouble and torment.

Miss Baker tells the story of a child of seven who stole some pennies from the pocketbook of another child. Her face wore a white, scared look during the morning. The pennies were missed. The teacher kept the child at noon having been haunted by her face during the session. The child confessed and was forgiven, but the white, drawn look still remained and was there to some extent the following two days, showing the persistence of the emotion.

The conscience that is not seared is a powerful ally for the right, but there is no subject upon which even Christian parents need more enlightenment than that of conscience. At birth the child possesses no standards of good and evil. His standards are formed entirely from his environment. If the environment has been good his first efforts to depart from it will be accompanied by pangs of conscience. He has that active tendency toward the conduct he has learned as good, so that he cannot take a step far from it without a struggle. Moreover his conduct is not so much what he has been taught but what he has observed. It is what the home and school spontaneously condemn or approve that gives the first and lasting content to conscience. Public opinion as expressed by parents and teachers becomes his standard of values, the measure of his conduct and the reach of his conscience. The conscientious child is the product of an atmosphere wherein "whatsoever things are lovely and of good report" are conveyed spontaneously.

The picture of right conduct through story will make a deeper impression upon the mind of a child than learning moral precepts. It is to be remembered that he thinks almost wholly in concrete terms. Precepts and laws are necessarily expressed in terms of abstract ideas while the conduct which the story pictures is concrete. Next to his need of being aided in making moral discriminations the child requires that the right, the good and the true be made attractive and desirable.

c. Precept and practice.

A child is now old enough to distinguish between what he is taught by precept and what he is taught by practice. Mental disorder and moral disaster are sure to result as soon as children discover inconsistencies in the lives of their parents and teachers. They are quick to discern any contradiction between the teacher of the word and the doer of the word. It is a fatal mistake to tell a boy about the horrors of a lie and then repudiate this instruction by deceiving the street car conductor respecting his exact age.

Clark was small for his age so when I bought tickets at the elevated station the lady took out only one fare. "He is of age," I said, "and should pay half-fare."

"Oh," she replied, "one would never know it from his size."

"Oh, but he knows it," I said, "and I would never want him to discover that his father had been untruthful."

Not many months later while driving to church one Sunday, the automobile stalled. I opened up the hood to examine the engine. "Oh, papa, you mustn't do that on Sunday!" So it was necessary to stop then and there and explain how everything had been in order the night before and that only some slight alteration would be necessary to enable us to get to church.

A child has every reason to believe that his teachers and parents practice what they preach, until he discovers that they do not. Sunday work, Sunday purchases and Sunday travel will contradict all the instruction that may be given him upon the sanctity of God's day. One exception to our general rule of life may be sufficient to upset his mental and moral equilibrium.

Miss Harrison tells the story of a small boy whose mother sent him from the table one night to wash his hands. "James," she said, "why do you come to the table with dirty hands when I always send you to wash them?"

"Once you didn't, mother," was the boy's quick rejoinder. He had been counting on that possibility every night when he took the chance.

Parents and teachers may be inconsistent in sins of omission as well as of commission. It is useless to teach a child to pray if we do not pray ourselves. H. S. McCowan, the author of *The Trail a Boy Travels*, says that it was overhearing his father in prayer one night that conclusively convinced him his father really cared for his soul. The value of the family altar is that the child sees and hears the parent pray as he has been taught to pray.

Church and Sunday-school attendance is another matter in which actions speak louder than words. Parents may urge their children to attend these services, but when a boy discovers father and mother are asking him to do something they will not do themselves, the whole inconsistency is apparent, and that is the end of the boy. While preaching a series of evangelistic sermons in my church I noticed that a young man was very much affected. Later on he made a public confession of his faith in Jesus Christ. Being interested to know what had been said that had led to his decision, I took him aside and inquired which one of my sermons had induced him to become a Christian.

"Oh, nothing I ever heard you say. It was the way my mother lived."

The child discriminates so quickly between precept and practice that it is of the greatest importance to remember, "What you do speaks so loudly that he cannot hear what you say." Thomas S. McPheeters, for years chairman of the Missouri State Committee, was once approached by one of his fellow church members with the request, "I wish you would speak to my boy on the subject of religion."

"Why don't you speak to him yourself?"

"I can't."

"Why not?"

"Because my boy is on to me."

"Well then," said Mr. McPheeters, "the best thing

you can do is to make a clean breast to your boy and quit your inconsistent living.''

4. Training.

The primary child is still hungry for a story so this remains as the teacher's best method of imparting instruction. Professor Hall says, ''Let me tell the story and I do not care who writes the text-books,'' while Professor James designates good story telling as one of the best intellectual qualifications of the teacher. The graded lessons abound in suitable stories for the primary child and lay the foundation for a chronological study of the Bible in the Junior department.

In addition to this method and material there should be training in

a. *Manual activity.*

Statistics state that one-third of the boys and girls of six can tie an ordinary double knot in a shoestring. At the age of seven the proportion is increased to two-thirds, while by the time the ninth year is reached practically all children can accomplish this task within fifteen seconds. This indicates the growing usefulness of the hands and the opportunity of developing this avenue of mental and spiritual expression. Home, school and church should provide a place for manual activity in their program. A small set of simple tools and a work bench, with plenty of drawing paper and crayons, are a valuable acquisition to the home, while a blackboard with simple designs for copying will provide opportunity both for entertainment and expression. Charles Inkenberry, in *Modes and Expression in Religious Education*, makes many suggestions for handwork in the Primary department. If ample time and accommodations cannot be provided in the Sunday-school for manual activity the Daily Vacation Bible School sessions should be utilized. If the summer school provides nothing more for our boys and girls than opportunities for religious expression, it is worth all the effort and the expense that it incurs.

b. Comprehensive worship.

As a little child he was led to worship through imitation and instruction, but now his understanding of God should promote his action. His capacity to know God has greatly increased as his world has enlarged and his experience broadened. The child needs God to account for many mysteries which arise from his widened field of observation. God as Creator and kind Heavenly Father, is the most satisfactory explanation. As yet he cannot appreciate God as the Triune Being or Christ as a personal Saviour. His interpretation of God is in the light of man with human hands to bless and of Christ as the perfect Man. It would be unwise to try to change his human conception of God and Christ if it only mystifies and confuses him. His religious sense will be normal when he petitions his Heavenly Father as he asks privileges from his earthly parents. When his capacity for reasoning develops, it will be easy to build upon these elementary conceptions the doctrine of divine sovereignty and salvation. Where faith continues unbroken it will be only a year or so before he can be brought to feel a sense of sin and his need of a Saviour.

Saving faith, however, must be comprehensive faith and a forced development in that early stage may mean an arrested development at a later stage. The fundamental purpose of all religious education in middle childhood is to prepare for the all-important decision that must be made in later childhood. Because a little child cannot comprehend God in the same relationship as a mature adult, does not mean that his God-given spirit of worship should not be encouraged. God to him is an unseen Companion, a faithful Friend. He can talk freely to Him but always with respect, for He is so great and powerful. He likes to have us tell Him things for He is always interested in His children. He gives us many things, especially health, so we must remember to thank Him. It grieves Him when we do wrong. He has commands for us just as parents have and He has commands for them, too, since they are also His children.

The church should mean more to the child than a tedious service. He should be taught to regard church attendance as a privilege and to appreciate something of the service. Before he attends a service of worship it might be well to show him the building and explain the purpose of the pulpit, the organ, the windows. It might be associated not only with parents and close relatives, but also with the apostles and martyrs and Christ himself. His understanding can also be furthered by teaching him hymns that will be sung, as well as a prayer of devotion that he can silently offer when he first takes his seat. Even the sermon may contain some simple truth within his comprehension which can be enlarged upon later by his parents. It is needless to say that church worship will have little significance to the children of this age unless they are accompanied by their parents. Hence it is important to secure the co-operation of the latter.

It is necessary for the Primary department to provide an adequate program of worship during the Sunday-school session.

c. Reverence.

One of the greatest problems of the Sunday-school is to secure the right attitude of the scholar to the holy things with which he is associated, and this problem can be solved if the proper emphasis is placed upon certain fundamentals in the very beginning. Much depends upon what impression the scholars form at first contact. It is interesting to note that Catholic children manifest deep reverence for their institutions because that attitude has been drilled into them from the very beginning. Reverence for God's day, for God's house and for God's ministers should be instilled into the heart and head of the child in the earliest years. This can be furthered by

(1) Order.

"Order is heaven's first law." This must dominate every session of the Sunday-school and every period of worship or lesson study. If a child finds chairs disarranged and books and papers on the floor, he will probably leave them so. The noisy superintendent may expect a noisy school. The first act of discipline which the superintendent or teacher performs should be upon herself. Order is as contagious as disorder. An orderly program, an orderly atmosphere and an orderly arrangement of things is sure to produce a deep feeling of respect. It is quite as much the business of the Sunday-school to instill reverence for God as it is to teach certain biblical facts regarding God. The word "discipline" literally means disciple(ing) or training in orderliness, and if we are to make boys and girls disciples of Jesus Christ, order must be the first requisite.

(2) Regularity.

A child's respect for an institution will also be in

proportion to that degree of regularity with which he has attended it. The importance of the church and Sunday-school is sure to suffer in his eyes just as soon as he detects any carelessness or indifference on the part of adults toward his attendance and punctuality. His whole spiritual welfare may hinge upon the attitude of parents to these matters. In many of our states boys and girls attend Sunday-school only half the time, and yet their parents wonder why they are lacking in regard for sacred things and so woefully ignorant of religious knowledge. Child crime has now reached appalling proportions in the United States and it cannot be curbed until parents have a new realization of their responsibilities. Reverence and respect for the church is only possible where in early life its services are attended with the same degree of regularity as are the sessions of the public school.

In conclusion it may be said that the greatest asset a teacher in the Primary department can possess is a *winning personality*. Her ability to attract children to herself means more now than at any other period of their life. The child now imitates the doer rather than the deed. He imagines who he would like to be when he is grown up and a winsome teacher is not unlikely to be his ideal. Winning the child to herself is the first step to winning him for Christ. "The best way for a child to learn to fear God," said Pestalozzi, "is to see and know a real Christian." The testimony of many a child convert has been as follows: "First I learned to love my teacher, then I learned to love my teacher's Bible, then I learned to love my teacher's Saviour."

But the problem of winning a child is not the same as that of instructing him. The child's attitude toward people depends upon the way he feels about them.

Dislike of religion is often directly traceable to the fact that religion in early childhood was associated with people who were strongly disliked. The teacher therefore cannot hope to win the child for any cause until she has won him to herself. To be a soul-winner she must first of all be a child-winner. This cannot be accomplished by threats or by making them afraid, nor can he be won merely by an expression of our love. More can be accomplished by entering into his life and sharing with him in the things that to him are of first importance. Time spent in playing with the child, in helping him in those directions in which he wishes for assistance, in endeavoring to understand his point of view, is not wasted. Adults know that it is essential to woo a woman if she is to be won. It is just as important that we win a child's confidence and regard in order to secure his compliance with our wishes. This does not mean that an adult is to play at being a child. A man does not woo or win a woman by pretending to be a woman. The adult who wins the child does so by remaining an adult, but he endeavors to understand the child. For the childish adult the child has only contempt, and once a child is prejudiced against a person, not only will his influence be lessened but it is quite likely that the child will act contrary to his suggestions.

---

1. Why is middle childhood a transition period?
2. In what three ways does the play of middle childhood differ from that of early childhood?
3. What kind of toys should be provided for children of this age?
4. What is the educative value of work?
5. What is the social value of work?
6. What is the moral value of work?
7. How is crime related to habits of work?
8. What is the law of apperception?

9. Why should a Sunday-school teacher visit the public school grades attended by her scholars?

10. What physical defects may impair the powers of observation during this period?

11. What three great discriminations does the child make in the religious realm?

12. Is the Santa Claus myth ever justifiable?

13. Why should Bible characters be presented now as we eventually expect to teach them?

14. How may a conscientious child be produced?

15. How do inconsistent lives affect both the mind and the morals of little children?

16. Why does the family altar and the family pew have so much to do with the prayer and church life of the child?

17. Why must Primary teachers be good story tellers?

18. What suggestions would you make for handwork in the Primary department?

19. What is the little child's comprehension of God and how may he worship Him with understanding?

20. What are two requisites for training in reverence?

21. What is the responsibility of parents for regular attendance in Sunday-school?

22. What is the greatest asset of the teacher in the Primary department?

23. What is the testimony of many a child convert as to steps that led to his conversion?

24. What does it mean to *win* a child?

Later Childhood

"From a child thou hast known the
holy scriptures."—2 Timothy 3:15.

XII

LATER CHILDHOOD

LATER childhood is one of the most interesting and
most important periods of life. It is called the
adult period of childhood, for the maturity of
the first division of life is reached and the child is at
his best physically, mentally and spiritually. Before he
enters into the second stage of life he must experience
as it were, a new birth and undergo great changes that
will affect his entire being.

Leavell has characterized the representative of later
childhood as energetic and independent, with verbal
memory at its height and an enlightened faith which
presents the greatest evangelistic opportunity.

McKinney in treating the Junior pupil gives a chapter to each of the following subjects: "The Reading
Age," "The Receptive Age," "The Memory Forming
Age," "The Curious and Imitative Age," "The Habit
Forming Age," "The Submissive and Fruitful Age."
While early adolescence may be regarded as the most
difficult period, later childhood perhaps is the most important, especially in view of the fact that it holds
within its training the solution of many of the problems
of adolescence. In this fascinating study of the adult
child it is to be observed that

1. Physically he is a rover.

At certain seasons there surges through the veins of
the boy a strong impulse to break conventional bounds
of home and school. He longs for the great out-of-
doors and finds his keenest enjoyment in the pursuits

that lie close to nature. This wanderlust is a natural
impulse rather than a moral delinquency. Kline's study
of the motives of truancy reveal little intent toward
wrongdoing in such breaks from the restraint of home
and school. The underlying impulses for these roving
tendencies satisfy a natural need.

a. This is a period of health and hardihood.

Growth is very slow, almost at a standstill, but there
is a marked increase in weight. In three years the boy
gains twenty-nine per cent and the girl thirty-seven per
cent in weight. Abounding health and unlimited energy
contribute to a constitution that is almost impregnable
to disease. Statistics indicate that the power to resist
sickness is greater now than at any other period of life.
While the death rate in middle childhood is 10.2 per
thousand, in early adolescence 5.5, in later adolescence
9.0, it is now only 4.7. His good health and boundless
energy no longer needed for growth urge him on to an
enlarged field of activity.

Not only does he meet the rigors of nature well, but
he craves a certain amount of struggle with the elements. It is his delight to contend against the wild
wind, to battle with the storm and to sleep out in the
open. He desires to exercise his lungs as well as his
limbs and feels the confines and conventionalities of the
home too narrow for his boundless and boisterous activities. Thus his nomadic tendencies have a very strong
physical basis.

b. Love of nature.

He longs for the great out-of-doors. Fields and
forests beckon to him. Lee has called this the "big
Injun age" because in so many ways its representatives imitate the out-of-door life of the Indians.
Hunting, fishing and camping out in the open air have
a peculiar fascination. He is full of adventure and

finds in the woods and wilds a world as yet undiscovered.

This desire to commune with nature is a God-given instinct. Not only has God much instruction to impart from His book of nature, but it is evident that it was not His purpose that the population of the earth should be congested in cities. His plan was the scattering of men throughout the earth that all might directly partake of the benefits He graciously bestows in the soil, the sunshine and the showers. But man's purpose has been just the opposite. He wants the company of man even if he must in consequence sacrifice the personal contact and communion with God. The confusion of tongues at Babel was God's rebuke to congestion in cities.

Truancy is the boy's rebuke to confinement in pigeon-hole desks known as apartment houses. To try to house boys and girls during these years in a flat or tenement is as cruel as to pen up young colts in a stall. Children who are doomed to dwell in the city can satisfy the instinct of migration with winter hikes and summer camps. The Boy Scouts and Campfire Girls provide an out-of-door program that is well suited for this purpose, though these organizations exist largely for the adolescent age. As a busy pastor in a city church, the author found it difficult to provide frequent outings for his boys during the winter months. For this reason the vacation time was employed. He went with them as far away from civilization as possible, where there would be freedom from all conventionalities and social restraints. For six weeks home centered in a tent, with fishing, bathing, sailing and roaming through wood and field. The boys were willing to have their freedom curtailed the rest of the year as long as they could look forward to these days in the wilds where they could yell and tear around to their heart's content.

Sunday-school teachers can ingratiate themselves with

their pupils if they will plan for frequent excursions into the woods, especially in the summer months. In this connection it will be found best to have men teachers for the boys and women for the girls so they can enter more fully into their pastimes. A lady who had a fine class of Junior boys once asked the writer to take them out on a hike. "Why don't you take them yourself?"

"Oh," she said, "I am afraid they would ask me to climb a tree."

The teacher that can enter most completely into their life is the one that they will be most likely to regard as their ideal.

Here is a domestic recipe, published in *The Youth's Companion*, that all parents should try. Those who have used it report most satisfactory results. If you want to preserve children, follow these directions:

Take

> 1 large grassy field
> ½ dozen children
> 2 or 3 small dogs
> A pinch of brook and pebbles

> Mix children and dogs well together and put them in field, stirring constantly. Pour brook over pebbles; sprinkle field with flowers; spread over a deep blue sky and bake in the sun. When brown, remove and set to cool in a bathtub.

2. Mentally he is an investigator.

Observation is far more accurate and reason is beginning to assert itself, which together with a growing spirit of self-reliance, render the child an independent and inquisitive examiner. He has just as many questions to ask as in former years but he is now discovering new ways of answering his own questions. His investigations are characterized and assisted by

a. Collections.

One writer says that ninety per cent of all children collect one thing or another. At the age of ten any child may be gathering four or five different sorts of things at once. Boys are more apt to pick up natural objects while girls acquire household trinkets. The craze for picture cards, coins and stamps does not appear until the close of this period. On the whole there is little attempt at arrangement or classification, the size of the collection being the important matter. Keen competition is often manifested in this pursuit, as some have observed, in the zeal of different boys to secure the cards of all candidates at election time.

However, there is an educative value in these collections. Not only are the faculties of observation quickened but the foundation is laid for the gathering in later life, of specimens for scientific study. It has been well demonstrated that the knowledge of a natural science can be acquired far more readily in the field than in the library and that the habits of gathering information direct from nature can be formed in childhood. The instinct of the age to live close to nature can be utilized in furthering a study of its wonders.

b. Mechanical interests.

There is a passion for investigating machinery of all kinds. Mechanical toys will be enjoyed for a study of the principles that underlie their movement and their destruction is not wanton and wilful but rather for the purpose of reconstruction. Not only toys but watches and clocks are in danger, but if they have outlived their usefulness it is helpful rather than harmful for them to serve the mechanical inquisitiveness of this age. It is said that James Watt, the inventor of the steam engine, when only a child, took a watch apart and from a knowledge of the principles constructed a wooden one that kept good time. Railroad engines have a special attraction to boys in particular and electrical devices are of almost equal interest. Automobiles and radios also contain a fascination, and frequently boys of this age are more familiar than their parents with the operation of modern inventions. It is well not only to encourage the boy in his study but also to provide him with suitable material and tools that he may work out the ideas he has secured in his investigations. The scroll saw, with which it is possible to produce an endless variety of creations, will be found a most useful implement. These tools may later prove one of the important supplementary interests that are so needed to balance the adolescent and adult life.

c. Reading.

Now that he is beginning to read easily, books afford him a new field of investigation. The world of books is a very large one, and just how far an individual will enter and explore this accessible domain will largely depend upon what action is taken at this time. Reading with some children becomes more interesting than playing. Parents and teachers could not ask for any better opportunity than to provide for this natural hunger and to cultivate a taste for the best books. If a child finds nothing but the sensational newspaper to satisfy his daily cravings, not only will his literary tastes be depraved but also his life will be marred and moulded by the objectionable matter the press provides for the public to read.

Moreover, as is the case with all instincts, failure to encourage the reading habit at this time may result in its loss. Forbush says that the reading habit is by no means universal. The majority of boys and girls read only what is prescribed in school. It is said that ten per cent of the young people do forty per cent of the reading. There is a steady and rapid decline in the amount of reading during the last two years of the high school age, which Forbush attributes largely to home influence. In a home where there are no books and no discussion of books, the reading instinct tends to atrophy. On the other hand, book-loving parents unconsciously create book-loving children and the kind of books they place in the hands of their boys and girls will shape their interests and characters.

One of the first books that was given Francis to read was Dickens' *Child's History of England*. The little fellow became very much absorbed in it. He read it and reread it until it was worn out from constant use. It aroused a hunger for history and he eagerly devoured the history and biography then so willingly placed in his hands. At the age of thirteen he received Thackeray's complete works for a present. *Vanity Fair* now became his inseparable companion and the sampler of a taste he was to acquire for the best fiction. It was not surprising, then, to discover a few years later that in history and literature his information was considerably in advance of his contemporaries in high school.

It is a mistake to regard a child's reading as a mere pastime. Whether he ever gets into the great world of books and draws mental and moral refreshment from its innumerable fountains, will depend upon his first impressions. Good books have always made great men. To the end of life the love of good literature will be one of its mightiest spiritual forces, so that the Sunday-school teacher as well as the parent has a responsibility in cultivating a taste for books. Boys read more in the field of action, girls in that of emotion. Boys are attracted mostly to travel and history, and girls to poetry and fiction. Both boys and girls, however, can be attracted to the Bible when once they are shown that it is a great composite of many books containing both action and emotion, prose and poetry, history and parable.

d. Memory.

Investigations in this period are of unusual value because the memory is acute. In fact this is often called the golden age of memory. Boys and girls at the age of twelve can remember nearly twice as much of a story as they could at the age of nine. Girls memorize more readily, boys more permanently, probably from the fact that girls are more inclined to learn by repetition and boys by association. Dr. Colegrove finds that boys have a better memory for descriptions and logical processes, while girls remember novel occurrences and single impressions. A good memory, however, is not an accident. A child will be accurate just in proportion as he is deeply impressed by some instruction or incident. Unless careful attention is given to an occurrence there is quite likely to be inaccuracy in its narration. The old adage, "Attention is the stuff that memory is made of," holds true at this point. And the key to all attention is interest. Because the world is so full of interest to the boy and girl of this age is one of the reasons why they remember so well. Certain it is, the facts he now learns are retained better than ever before, and almost better than ever again. An old man will vividly recall incidents in his boyhood days when more stirring events in later life have completely faded.

Children employ two methods for memorizing:

(1) Repetition.

"Line upon line and precept upon precept," depending upon brute repetition rather than attentive thought to drive the thing home, was the particular plan used by the ancients, the Jews in particular, in their schools. It is still the method employed in the orient. Where education is regarded as merely the acquisition of knowledge, repetition is largely used to establish information.

(2) Association.

Incidents are fixed in mind through their association with familiar things. The law of apperception is applied to the memory. This prepares for the orderly laying away of all new experiences. It is the method of modern education and finds its greatest support in the occident.

During the past two decades a great change has taken place in our schools. Children now learn by association and action rather than by repetition. In practically all foreign countries the method of teaching consists mainly in requiring pupils to memorize the contents of books and recite them without verbal error. The "gymnasium" which European countries substitute for our high school, aptly suggests the mental discipline to which European children are subjected in their memory methods. While it is evident that in later life association and not repetition is the only practical method of memorizing, it is questionable whether it should be applied exclusively in the years of childhood.

Dr. Croswell noticed that children up to nine and ten do not have a very clear sense of the fitness of things and are apt to make inappropriate associations. Reason is still far from being developed and it is only too evident that there are many things a child could profitably store up in his mind without full comprehension. Then there is the mental discipline which all memorizing provides. There is no question that an adult can learn much more readily by association if he has had the drill of repetition in childhood. The mental discipline in repetition which has not been regarded as drudgery in childhood has prepared the mind to absorb more readily in later life. Mental discipline like physical exercise is essential to growth, and in the modern trend to make learning easy and interesting, parents and teachers should not go to the opposite extreme and discard whatever is not of natural and easy interest to the child. Children can be put down to hard work and required to do their work well, provided the sessions are not too long, the work too advanced and the physical strain too great.

As memory is stronger than reason at this time, arts rather than sciences should occupy the largest place in the educational program. It cannot be said that the American plan of promoting mathematics instead of languages in the years of childhood is an improvement upon the method still adhered to in European schools. Children born on the foreign field, even when educated in their own country, have a far better grasp of the language of their childhood than the missionaries who make it a special study in later life. It is also true that missionaries from European countries generally excel American missionaries in their command of oriental languages. On the other hand, it has been proven that mathematics can be more readily mastered after the mind has been disciplined in linguistic study.

3. Socially he is a gangster.

There is a striking tendency among animals to herd or band together that finds its counterpart in the in-

stincts of the human race. Even the most benighted
tribes live in groups more or less organized. Solitude
is feared and shunned by all human beings. The desire
for the presence of others shows itself even in babies,
and is manifested in the formation of groups or gangs
in the later years of childhood. This is furthered by

a. Dislike of the opposite sex.

Boys and girls from nine to twelve no longer share
the same interests or enjoy the same games. Boys get
a dislike for the quieter ways of the girl, while girls
can see nothing refined in the boisterous, bullying boy.
Miss Whitley says, "By ten or eleven a boy is learning
lessons of group loyalty which the girl learns with
greater difficulty. Certain petty jealousies remain as a
dividing force, hindering the co-operation of the girls'
group as a unit. Girls group themselves more often in
the winter time for social rather than athletic ends.
These might better be designated as 'sets' rather than
gangs. The set is exclusive and undemocratic. It has
no organization, leader or history. It snubs its rivals
while the gang fights them. The members of a set also
snub one another and quarrel among themselves. There
is none of the deep-seated instinctive loyalty which the
members of the gang have for each other."

b. Tendency for organization.

The gang or set is very loosely organized but it is
the first step in this direction. Boys and girls find they
can accomplish more by organized effort or team work
and this becomes an underlying motive fully as much
as the desire for company. Dr. Sheldon's study of
children's groups gives us some very interesting information. Of more than one thousand boys from ten to
sixteen it was discovered that eight hundred and fifty-
one belonged to organizations of some kind. Sixty-one

per cent of these were athletic, in fact, it was noted that physical activity was the keynote to the greatest number. The most groups were formed at the ages of eleven, twelve and thirteen. Girls and boys organize in different ways. Girls form five times as many social societies as boys, twice as many philanthropic and three times as many secret, industrial and literary. On the other hand, boys form four times as many out-of-door societies and seven times as many athletic clubs as the girls. Girls are more nearly governed by adult motives than boys. They organize to promote sociability, to advance their interests, to improve themselves and others. Boys are more like savages. They associate to hunt, fish, roam, fight and to contest physical superiority with each other.

Parents and teachers cannot ignore the gang and its influence over their boys and girls. Instead they must seek to get into its good graces and influence the character of what goes on without a realization on the part of children that there is any interference with their activities. If a gang can be made to suppress its own lawlessness and become the protector of those upon whom it has been preying, what limit is there to the utilization of its spirit and enthusiasm?

The gang is usually subject to its leader and he therefore should be the first object in any campaign to win the favor and support of the group. When the gang constitutes a Sunday-school class regular attendance and interest is assured. Happy is the teacher who can make his class the baseball team that claims the loyalty and interest of each member.

4. Spiritually he is a worshiper.

In early years he imitated persons but not as ideals. In later life he will conceive ideals but not in persons.

Now all his ideals are represented in some known character. His hero is very real to him. Boys find their heroes in everyday life. Girls are more likely to obtain them from books. Boys invariably place men upon their pedestal, but girls are likely to find their ideals in either a man or a woman.

The first heroes are men of physical achievement. The star pitcher and the dashing halfback are in danger of worship. Indeed few athletes realize what influence they now possess. A Christian football player who has won the admiration of the boy can easily win his will. While the writer was a pastor in Japan a member of the New York National Baseball Team was sent over to coach the Waceda University team. The young man appeared at church Sunday morning and later accepted an invitation to address the boys of Palmore Institute. No speaker ever commanded closer attention than this baseball player and no message was ever more carefully chosen. Instead of telling the boys how to play baseball he spoke of the promise he had made to his mother never to smoke nor drink nor neglect his Bible and his church. "I attended the Union Church last Sunday," he said, "because I am a Christian and a church member and have never failed to respect my mother's wishes."

Hero worship need not necessarily be confined to men who perform striking, dramatic physical exploits. The reason that the circus clown, the football celebrity and the movie star are the first to come into the life of the child, is because of the absence of anything better. A boy always longs to place his father on the throne of his heart if he is given a chance, but most fathers of today are not willing to get into the life of their boy sufficiently to merit this honor. A child may be brought into contact with better ideals. Wise parents will make it a point to entertain missionaries in their home, and schools will solicit the presence of men of national reputation for what effect it will have in shaping the ideals of the children. Where care is exercised as to contacts a child's hero may be good as well as great.

The heroes of history, of literature, and of the Old Testament may be brought out through the story and through the child's own reading. Nowhere can be found such a hall of fame as in the Bible. What boy will not become intensely interested in the experiences of Joseph and the exaltation of Daniel? What girl will not be captivated by the courage and success of Esther? The reason that such a small per cent of children choose Bible characters as their ideals is because these have never been so vividly presented as have less worthy personalities. The graded lessons of the Sunday-school have recognized this trend and the hero stories provided, set forth the best ideals for the boys and girls of the Junior department.

As all Roman roads led to the imperial city, so all Bible ideals should lead to Christ. Jesus is the Hero of heroes. The culmination of all hero lessons will be to bring the children to find their ideal in Christ. As the Old Testament characters are in so many instances types of the coming Messiah, so all hero lessons should be stepping stones to the Hero of all heaven and earth.

5. Training.

These are the golden years of opportunity. With his health at its best and his understanding now capable of grasping the serious and solemn matters of life, the adult child possesses a world of possibilities. Now, while he is artless, docile and trustful he must be firmly an-

ehored against the storm and stress that will shake his
soul in the trying and troublesome teens. Upon the
foundation of habits of clean thinking and right living,
built up in these and preceding years, will the house
stand firm when the doubts, the rebellions and the ro-
mantic imaginations of adolescence appear. Fortunate
is he if he carries with him a faith in the goodness and
love of God and in Jesus Christ as his Saviour and
Keeper, with relations to the church, Sunday-school,
Bible and prayer that are so firmly cemented as not to
be easily broken. To further this end special attention
should be given to

a. *The use of the Sabbath.*

Sunday ought to be the

"Day of all the week the best"

and always associated with the happiest memories.
While it may be a day of real rest for grown people, to
the child it should be a day of change. Many simple
innovations make Sunday a festival to children and
create happy and lifelong memories. For their intense
physical needs change in the food and in the table fur-
nishings are quickly observed. Clean clothes and everything that is new and best should appear on Sunday.
One reason why church-going is wholesome is because
it counteracts the personal slovenliness that usually belongs to those who are "porch" Christians.

At church a program of information, worship and expression should occupy much of his time. At home
Bible books and Bible games should be preserved for
Sunday and Sunday only. It is just as serious a mistake to permit what is appropriate for Sunday to become
common by use during the week as it is to permit week
day practices to become cursed by introducing them on

Sunday. Clark was more interested in the reading of *Pilgrim's Progress* than anything else. But he was not permitted to read this excellent book except on Sunday and only a chapter of it at a time. This preserved his interest and enabled him to look forward to every Sunday afternoon with eager anticipation.

There is no greater detriment to the sanctity of the Sabbath than the Sunday newspaper. By the time the church bell rings Sunday morning, in many homes the whole family is buried in the blanket sheets of a Sunday newspaper. In fact, one newspaper does not contain enough sporting news to go around, so two papers have been purchased and the comic supplement is the children's favorite. I recently asked a reporter why they did not have more room for religious news. He replied what people want is scandal, murder or some crime sensation. Thus this common sewer of our social life, this cesspool of shames and scandals, has become the Sabbath legacy of the parents for their children. Do you wonder that boys grow up to find heroes in criminals, and girls in depraved women, when such a diet is dished for their mental and moral digestion every Sabbath?

b. The use of the Bible.

As the teacher is the central figure in the Primary department, the Bible should occupy a similar place in the Junior department. Having won the child to herself the next object of the teacher should be to win him to God's Word. A copy of the Bible should now be placed in his hands as his personal property. The idea of providing Bibles for use only in Sunday-school at this age when children crave to have possessions of their own, is not likely to quicken an interest in the Book of books. Moreover it is a mistake to select editions of the Scriptures printed in smaller type than the child is accustomed to read. A Bible with flexible leather binding with its contents printed in large type and illustrated with attractive pictures may become the brightest cornerstone of the future library. Shorter Bibles are not recommended since the omissions may lead the child in later life to believe that they were of less relative importance. The danger that he will come across passages which are unsuitable for his reading need not be exaggerated since the possibility is that the child will not understand their meaning and therefore will probably skip them.

Every boy and girl of this age, then, should have his own Bible, and parent and teacher can do much to help them become familiar with its arrangement by books, chapters and verses as well as the content of its narratives.

Competitive drills in looking up references are a pleasant and profitable exercise. Where this is continued faithfully the child can turn to any portion of Scripture almost immediately. The study of the lesson should be conducted with Bible in hand, although care should be taken that interest is not sacrificed through excessive reading of difficult and incomprehensible passages. In the reading of *Pilgrim's Progress* Clark was eager to look up the references, provided the number and length did not detract from his interest in the story.

c. Memory work.

As at no other time will the child be able to absorb so much and remember so well, his mind should be stored with spiritual truths from which he can draw upon in the emergencies of the future. Hymns, psalms and choice selection as well as facts regarding Bible geography and history should be accurately committed to memory. Much that is not now understood will be revealed to the larger reason in later experience and will present a bulwark of strength against the coming storms of temptation and doubt. Even the conquest of the much despised catechism will be appreciated in later life. Young men being examined for ordination to the ministry have found it was not the theological knowledge acquired in seminary so much as their remembrance of the catechism learned in childhood days that enabled them to give a ready answer to all questions.

d. *Experience and training in worship.*

It is generally accepted that the habit of attending public worship should be formed in childhood or it will be difficult to make the young adolescent a participant. It is coming to be acknowledged that if the child be present he should be made to feel that he is both wanted and welcomed and part of the services should be adapted to his understanding and arranged for his participation. A children's hymn, prayer and address can be introduced without lowering the tone of worship. Children do not require silly sermons or senseless songs. They will enjoy real worship if it is within their comprehension. Few ministers realize that simple sermons are always appreciated by adults. If theological students would study the art of telling Bible stories to children their sermons to adults would gain two hundred per cent in living interest. It was because adults crowded the church to hear "Charlie" Spurgeon's talks to children that he was led to enlarge his field without altering the simplicity of his address.

When Clark was ten he was given a copy of Wright's *Six Minute Sermons for Children* with the suggestion that he read one every Sunday afternoon. After several weeks the idea of preaching this sermon presented itself. To this his father agreed upon condition that he would memorize it. For some time afterwards in the early evening the family gathered in reverent attention while the little fellow carried out his service of song, Scripture, sermon and prayer.

Where the parents cannot be interested in the maintainance of a family pew, special provision should be made for the child's worship, either through the combined church and Sunday-school or the inauguration of a children's church.

e. Decision and church membership.

Professor Athearn in his most recent investigations of 6,194 individuals from twenty-six different states, discovered that the peak of conversion is now at the thirteenth year. It is needless to say that as the child enters his twelfth year teachers and parents should be confronted with the great responsibility of bringing him to personally and publicly accept Jesus Christ as his Saviour. As the teacher is the central figure in the sixth year and the Bible the outstanding object of the ninth year, so Christ, the center and circumference of all Scripture, should be the supreme topic of the closing days of childhood.

The ages of twelve and thirteen mark the first of three periods in life when the soul is most sensitive to the voice of God. Many would defer this all-important matter until the second or the third period. They argue that the greatest number of conversions take place in adolescence and that the youth is far more capable than the child of comprehending such a significant step. But such delay is often fatal. In dealing with children we are generally a year or so *too late*. The mere fact that eighty per cent of the boys and girls in the Sunday-school slip through our hands without making a decision for Christ, should convince us that the first impressionable period of evangelistic opportunity may be the last. Why sunset days in the golden age of childhood should be employed for evangelistic effort rather than stormy years of youth, may be seen from the following considerations:

(1) Twelve was an important age in Jewish life.

Canon Farrar says that according to Jewish legend it was at this age that Moses left the house of Pharaoh's daughter; Samuel heard the voice which summoned him to the prophetic office; Solomon gave the judgment which first reveals his wisdom; Josiah first dreamed his great reform. It was not surprising that Christ was found at this age with the learned doctors in Jerusalem. According to Jewish custom He had now become a *bar mitsvah,* "son of the law," and took upon Himself the personal responsibility of fulfilling the law. The Jewish age of accountability is strongly suggestive as most timely for Christian decision.

(2) Many great and good men date their conversion from childhood.

Polycarp, the aged martyr of the early church, has left it on record that he became a follower of Christ at the age of nine. Matthew Henry gives the age of ten as the date of his conversion. Isaac Watt accepted Christ when nine years old, while Jonathan Edwards dates the beginning of his Christian life from his seventh year. Out of seventy-one corporate members of the American Board of Missions, nineteen stated they were converted at so early an age that they were unable to remember, while thirty-four were led to Christ before they were fourteen.

(3) Childhood is followed by a period of temporary religious decline.

The simple faith of the child gives way to doubt, his confidence to mistrust and his confiding nature to reticence. The well known reserve that characterizes the adolescent causes him to hide much of his eager but secret interest in religion. The rise of the gang spirit tends to lessen the hold of teacher and parent. Above all, the physical changes through which he is now passing tend to unsettle him. It is surely better that before the stormy teens the young life should be firmly anchored in Christ and committed to His care, than that the frail bark should be launched upon the treacherous waves of adolescence without the firm hand of the Great Pilot on the helm.

(4) The great majority of boys and girls drop out of the Sunday-school during the days of early adolescence.

Perhaps the greatest failure of the Sunday-school is its inability to hold on to its scholars after they finish their childhood days. Sixty-five per cent of the girls and seventy-five per cent of the boys drift away to become the religious derelicts of the community. Only a very small proportion of them are brought back to the church through the revival.

(5) Child conversions are permanent conversions.

"The most surprising evidences of the permanent results of child conversion," says Rev. Lionel B. Fletcher, "are to be seen in any meeting where those present who were converted under the age of twelve years are asked to hold up their hands. Generally the proportion is so astonishing that any sane man must wonder how it is that people will continue to theorize instead of acting on the evidence of their own eyesight." Dr. Spurgeon confirms this fact in the following statement: "I have more confidence in the spiritual life of the children that I have received into this church than I have in the spiritual condition of the adults thus received. I will go even further than that. I have usually found a clearer knowledge of the gospel and a warmer love for Christ in the child convert than in the adult convert."

> (6) *Decisions for Christ in childhood prepare the way for other important decisions in adolescence.*

After making a careful study of 1,339 decisions which it has been possible for him to follow through a series of years, Dr. F. F. Peterson has reached these conclusions:

Win for Christ in the grammar school.

Secure life service decisions in high school.

Train for life service in college.

Not more than ten per cent of our grammar school pupils finish the high school and only a very small proportion reach college. A decision for Christ in childhood may not only inspire the adolescent to prolong his preparatory period, but also to make decisions for Christian service while there is still time and opportunity for adequate preparation.

---

1. Give some general characteristics of later childhood.
2. Why is this perhaps the most important of all periods?
3. Give two reasons why the boy is a rover.
4. Is truancy justifiable? What is the remedy?
5. Why should men teach boys in the Junior department?
6. Name four mental characteristics of this period.
7. What value is associated with a child's collections?
8. Why should mechanical investigations be encouraged?
9. Why should we "give attention to reading" during this period?

10. How may literary tastes be cultivated?
11. What two methods do children employ in memorizing?
12. Discuss the relative value of these two methods.
13. Why does the European missionary generally excel the American missionary in his command of oriental languages?
14. What two social characteristics attract the boy to the gang?
15. What are some of the differences between the organizations of boys and girls?
16. How should we deal with the gang?
17. Why is hero worship greater now than at any other period?
18. How can we help a child to select his heroes?
19. Why is later childhood the golden period of opportunity in training?
20. Make some suggestions as to a proper observance of the Sabbath.
21. What type of a Bible should be provided the Junior boy and how should he be taught to use it?
22. What memory work would you suggest?
23. What provisions for worship should be made?
24. What is the greatest responsibility that confronts the Junior teacher?
25. Give six reasons why the closing days of childhood should be employed for evangelistic effort.

Early Adolescence

"As thy servant was busy here and there, he was gone."—1 Kings 20:40.

XIII

EARLY ADOLESCENCE

A DOLESCENCE is a word that was not found in the dictionary a generation ago. It has remained for modern psychology to discover youth and set it apart as a life that has neither the characteristics of childhood nor the maturity of adulthood. Rousseau says, "We are born twice, the first time into existence and the second time into life; the first time a member of the race and the second time a member of the sex." To this we would add the great spiritual birth—the birth of the believer into the kingdom of God. These new births are the great characteristics of adolescence. However, adolescence is not a life entirely set apart by itself. Striking and distinctive as are its peculiar features they have their preparation in the preceding periods. "There is no characteristic of adolescence," says Tracy, "whose germ may not be found in childhood and whose consequences may not be traced in maturity and old age." Back of adolescence are boyhood and childhood, and back of childhood are the forces of heredity.

Adolescence is the great transition period. What takes place during adolescence may be ascertained by noting the difference between the child of twelve and the adult of twenty-four.

Physically the child is a framework, the adult a building.

Mentally the child is a pupil, the adult a personality.

Socially the child is a playmate, the adult a partner.

Religiously the child is an inquirer, the adult a believer.

The activity of the child gives way in adolescence to accomplishment and in adulthood to achievement. The play of the child passes into games, then athletics, and finally manifests itself in the active competition of life. The inquiring child becomes critical in adolescence, but proves sound in judgment in later life. The playmates of children give way to the companions and friendships of youth and later the confines of the social circle narrows to the most intimate relations. The credulity of little children yields to doubt and disagreement, which in turn lays the foundation for the strong convictions of the adult.

Children mark their approach to the adolescent life by accelerated growth, but the girl in addition gives evidences of her maidenhood by the new interest that she takes in her personal appearance. The boy, on the other hand, is no longer the credulous, boisterous child, for he manifests his entrance into youth by an attitude that is more quiet and reserved and less confidential.

Adolescence may be divided into two periods of four years each. Early adolescence would embrace the years from thirteen to sixteen, while later adolescence would include the years from seventeen to twenty. Strictly speaking, adolescence does not end with the twentieth year. While physical maturity may be possible at twenty-one this is not true of the intellectual, social and spiritual nature. Twenty-four is generally set as the extreme limit of adolescence, although the intense age in which we live has a tendency to accelerate rather than retard maturity. The majority of young people do not have a completed adolescence. The maturing process which proceeds slowly and gradually is only too often hastened by premature entrance upon life's responsibilities. Poverty, misfortune and sorrow will also terminate this era of development. While thirteen may be designated as the initial year of adolescence, climate and environment must be reckoned as factors in lengthening or shortening the period of childhood. Girls invariably enter into adolescent life at least a year earlier than boys.

Early adolescence may be compared to the early years of childhood when enlargement and growth are the order of things. Later adolescence, like later childhood, is a period of adjustment and consolidation. Early adolescence, however, in addition to assuming the burden of physical enlargement must likewise bear the storm and the stress that accompany the birth and development of the sexual functions. With the awakening of new powers within the adolescent and the stirring of adult aspiration, there is a turbulent mixture of tendencies and counter-tendencies. It is essential that the child become an adult, but this cannot be accomplished by any instantaneous transformation. Nevertheless new forces and influences are surging within the youth. He lived in one world in childhood. Now he must adjust himself to a very different world. He becomes conscious of many elements in human life which he had not known. He has a new social consciousness but has not outgrown the self-regard of childhood. He wants to believe like a child but be treated like a gentleman. Being neither a child nor a man, but having a mixture of the traits of childhood and manhood, he is a complex of contradictions. It is not strange that boys and girls of this age are misunderstood. Still less can we expect them to understand themselves. Until we realize that complexities and self-contradictory traits are the natural order of early youth, we are not prepared to deal intelligently and charitably with its eccentricities. It is well, then, to be informed as to the singularities that mark early adolescent life.

1. The principal physical characteristic is change.

The changes that take place at this period are important and fraught with great consequences. There is

a. Change in body.

From thirteen to fifteen there is a rapid but uneven growth. The growing power is not evenly distributed throughout the body and the danger of overexertion is evident. Girls grow faster between thirteen and fourteen, boys between fourteen and fifteen. Girls are slightly taller than boys at twelve and on into thirteen; slightly taller at fourteen and less at fifteen. For three years the girl is taller than the boy, but at sixteen fully two inches shorter. Girls are heavier than boys for two years, thirteen and fourteen, but lighter at all other times. By the fifteenth year both boys and girls have secured nine-tenths of their weight. The brain is nearly full size in later childhood, but the heart and lungs continue to grow late in adolescence. The heart nearly doubles in size and the lung capacity is greatly increased.

The struggle for control and mastery of the muscles in this age of rapid growth manifests itself in an awkwardness and ungainliness on the part of both boys and girls. Despite the unstable equilibrium of health that naturally results from these marked physical changes, the general vitality is high. In no other period of life except later childhood is the death rate so low.

b. Change in ideals.

The development of the sexual instincts influences his

ideals. He is no longer an imitator nor even a hero worshiper. According to Weigle, "His vision penetrates the outward act and catches the spirit within a man. He begins to discern inward qualities and to feel the intrinsic worth of truth, faith and self-sacrifice. He is full of ambitions and makes elaborate plans for the future." He will throw himself into some new interest with the utmost ardor but in a few weeks it will be forgotten. His ideals are fleeting and his decisions temporary. Lack of mature experience causes him to attempt the impractical if not the impossible, and arouses him from his day dreams to the stern realities of adolescent life. Happy is the youth who may now find a sympathizing friend in his father or teacher to awaken him from his dream without that manifestation of impatience that leaves in its wake a sense of regretful disillusionment. Many boys and girls whose youthful ideals have been harshly treated have built up a wall of defensive reserve that has separated their parents from their confidence.

c. Change in pursuits.

Day dreams of coming manhood together with the growing feeling of independence that is beginning to assert itself, creates a strong desire to go to work. School now loses its hold upon youth as the fascination of money-making grips him. Thorndike has shown that the tendency to drop out of school is greatest in the last two years of the elementary grades and the first years of high school. The tragedy of youth is that eighty-five per cent of its representatives in this early period predestine their life work. One of the greatest handicaps to all classes today is that ninety per cent of the people have entered blindly or accidentally upon their present employment irrespective of their fitness for it.

The old plan by which a young man was apprenticed to an artisan until he was of age was infinitely better than the youthful independence of the present day, which permits boys and girls to launch out upon the strong, turbulent ocean of life with their craft but half-constructed, half-equipped and half-manned.

d. Change in disposition.

Rapid and uneven development of body is responsible for the frequent changes of mood that characterize early youth. His days are marked by irregularities and extremes. At one time he manifests activity, at another apathy. One day he is hilarious and the next despondent. In the morning he may be moved by generous impulses, but by afternoon he is actually greedy. One hour he is astonishingly self-conceited, but the next he manifests marked feelings of timidity. To judge his actions on one occasion, he might be considered exceedingly virtuous, but a little later such fond hopes are shattered by the exhibition of a vicious disposition.

These eccentricities manifest themselves in other ways. Likes and dislikes are exceedingly strong. Favorite foods are often indulged in to excess. Others are positively loathed. It is an age of intense craving. Tracy says, "The appetite seeks what is stimulating to the taste, the muscles cry out for strenuous exertion, and the mind for a story with an exciting plot. Hence intemperance is apt to show itself and unless checked fix itself as a life habit." Sexual and social temptations are intensified by the fact that at this period the youth is poorly prepared to resist. Moderation even in athletics is hard to observe, while late hours and the strain of the social engagements of an intense age are apt to impair the physical vigor at the very time of life when rapid physical development demands conservation rather than expenditure of energy.

To understand these irregularities and weaknesses of adolescence is of the highest importance for parent and teacher. Once recognizing and realizing the scope of these contradictory impulses the actions of a single day should never discourage or satisfy any instructor of youth. Judgment must be reserved for a longer acquaintance and no character considered established until this transition period is complete. The boy who is inattentive in Sunday-school today will surprise you by his interest next Sunday and you will have reason to reverse your opinion of him. If we judge boys and girls of this age by adult standards they will ever prove a puzzle, but when we exhibit a hopeful and sympathetic disposition to a nature that we recognize as changeable, our counsel and companionship will be of the utmost value. Youth cannot be driven, but he may be tactfully directed in health and in habits of deep breathing, bathing, eating, sleeping and abundant exercise.

Since youth is never calm it behooves his leaders to continually present a placid and patient disposition, mingled with a spirit of charity and humor. There is nothing like an atmosphere of regularity and a calm and even environment to modulate this excitable and eccentric nature, strengthen it against temptation and store up reserve powers for the days to come.

2. The principal mental characteristic is criticism.

Adolescence is by far the most critical period in the entire life of the individual. Coming into prominence in early youth is a direct consciousness of one's ability to solve problems and a growing insistence upon sub-

mitting all things to the test of one's reason. In childhood things were accepted upon faith, but now faith is
yielding to reason and all authority will be questioned
and criticized. According to Burr, "Not only does the
boy assert his own ideas with great freedom, but he
challenges those of others. To some anxious adults he
seems to have no respect for God or man. He is ready
to take a shot with his critical pop-gun at time-honored
creeds or well established social customs." No one need
be disturbed by this natural tendency to question matters credulously accepted by children and experimen-
tally settled by adults. It is criticism in adolescence
that leads to conviction in adult life. To become a
man he cannot always have a guardian at his elbow de-
ciding for him. Moreover criticism is the basis of individual thought, and neither personality nor progress
would be possible in a realm where there is fixed confidence in prevailing conditions and beliefs. Truth will
only be strengthened by criticism and it is the inalienable right of every growing mind to demand proofs.

The critical attitude of this period is not a negation
by any means. Such more positive doubt may appear
in later adolescence, but now there is simply a demand
for reasons. If a negative attitude is adopted it is because we have tried to silence this spirit of criticism.
Indeed it is quite possible by pressing our authority at
a time when reason is sought, to force youth into doubt
and disputation. Burr says, "History gives us plentiful
illustrations of what happens when authority becomes
papal in religion and imperial in politics and the critical
faculty is crushed. We have no excuse for making such
a blunder in either secular or religious education."

The critical disposition of the adolescent indicates that
he has now entered into a new era of mental development. While physical habits were formed in childhood,

mental habits may be established in youth. Childhood presents the mental capacity to acquire, adolescence provides the capacity to think. Boyhood presents the personality to ask, adolescence provides the will to act. For this reason

a. *Adolescent education should include a wide variety of subjects.*

It is characteristic of youth that new interests emerge with great suddenness, and devotion to any one study is often short-lived. This ought not to be disconcerting to parent or teacher when reminded that this is the time for tasting and sampling a great variety of subjects. The wider the mental horizon is extended in youth the more life will have to offer in later years. Youth is to be prepared for living as well as for working and the multiplications of his interests in the teens will enrich and ennoble his life in the twenties and thirties.

Failure in one interest may be counteracted by success in another. It is only by passing our critical student through the entire realm of knowledge that his inclinations and interests may be revealed. When the writer had reached the teen age his mother took him out under the starry heavens and by her knowledge and enthusiasm cultivated within him a deep interest in astronomy. Every text upon this subject was read with eagerness, amateur experiments followed and at the age of eighteen he was writing astronomical articles for various publications. At an early age this far-seeing parent likewise launched her son into the realms of vocal and instrumental music and his interests were so multiplied and intensified in later adolescence that there was neither time nor desire for questionable amusements that some feel are almost indispensable to the life of young people. The more pursuits in which we

can interest a boy in the early teens the less attention
will he give to the frivolities of the later teens.

> *b. Adolescent education should deal with knowl-
> edge en masse.*

Neither his instruction nor his examination should
be upon detailed information, but the object should be
to provide general impressions and fundamental principles in just as large a field as possible. Progress may
be hindered rather than helped by an over-exacting
examination system. Just now the receptive instincts
are far ahead of the creative and expressive powers.
Generalization should be the program of early adolescence, *specialization* that of later adolescence. Teachers
must be neither under-equipped nor over-equipped.
The poorly trained teacher can neither interest nor instruct and is sure to reveal his incompetence. On the
other hand, a scholarly instructor is in danger not only
of overestimating the preparatory knowledge of the
pupil, but also of destroying his interest through giving
abnormal attention to details.

> *c. Intellectual capacities that are not started or
> stimulated in early adolescence may be lost.*

The child's acquisition of knowledge when arrested or
terminated in adolescence tends to atrophy. The ability
to read or to study may from neglect in adolescence be
lost entirely. To interrupt a child's mental growth at
this time may rob him of much that he has already acquired. "To him that hath shall be given, but to him
that hath not shall be taken away even that which he
hath." New languages are practical and possible to
adults only so far as the foundation of language construction has been laid at this time. If a boy becomes
acquainted with a musical instrument in the teens and

takes sufficient lessons to develop the fundamental co-
ordination of nerve and muscle, he may successfully
revive his music in later life. But adult life possesses
only the improvement of such capacities as have been
cultivated in the early years. This principle has the
very widest application both in the world of mind and
the world of morals. All the foundations, then, for the
large range of possible achievements and enjoyments of
later life must be laid or strengthened during these all
important years. For this reason our educational work
must be extensive, that every possible channel of mental
activity may be explored.

3. The principal social characteristic is companion-ship.

The gang in which the child in his last years finds
the outlet for his social instincts, reaches the peak of
its prominence in the thirteenth year and then declines.
This does not indicate that the youth is becoming less
social, but rather that his social life is being shaped by
new instincts and interests. The fact that he now
realizes he is no longer a member of the race but a
member of the sex gives birth to such characteristics
as altruism and self-sacrifice, which are primarily parental instincts. However these instincts are only in
the formative period and there continues those alterna-
tions and contradictions that so strongly designate this
paradoxical period. There exists side by side a desire
for solitude as well as for society and a self-assertion
that at times overshadows the new consciousness of loyal
devotion to others. There is also a desire for public
approbation that is strongly tempered by a feeling of
shyness. In no place are these contending impulses
more strongly marked than in the attitude manifested
toward the opposite sex. For the first two years of

adolescence the sex-repulsion that characterized later childhood prevails and if anything, is even more pronounced. There is a complete change of attitude, however, in the middle years of adolescence and sex-repulsion gives way to sex-attraction. "Boys begin to pay attention to their dress and girls are no longer tomboys."

It is evident that a parent or teacher must have tact and understanding to deal with these various impulses. A word of encouragement at the right time may be far-reaching, while unthinking criticism may destroy confidence. Too much consideration cannot be given to social contacts as controlling influences of adolescence. Where religious convictions are not predominant, youth is generally controlled by public or gang opinion, the influence of friends and the judgment of recognized leaders. His counsellors and companions, then, are of the greatest importance in shaping his life. For this reason it will be well to consider

a. Companionship in the home.

Home is the primary social unit because it is the group of persons with the widest disparity of age, experience, ability and wisdom, united by an equality of affection and a conviction of each other's supreme worth. But youth does not always have companionship in the home. Blind, blundering parents, ignorant of the complex, contending impulses are apt to misjudge and misunderstand. The young lad who now feels the vigor of manhood cannot tolerate being treated as a child. This is not the time for scolding or nagging, and pious advice and petty punishment are worse than useless. At no other time is the divine injunction more to be heeded, "Fathers, provoke not your children to wrath."

Parents must recognize the growing spirit of independence which is as natural to this stage as dependence is to the child. To repress it is to invite lasting weakness, or constant friction and ultimate lack of control. Adolescent opinions and objections must be respected and not repelled. Gradually rule by authority must give way to rule by reason, and sound judgment can be developed only by exercise and experience. The resentment that the adolescent manifests toward authority does not indicate that he has less reverence and regard for his parents. On the other hand there is a growing interest in adult life and a new craving for the companionship of elders. Fortunate is the boy whose father is now willing to become his close counsellor and companion. The Roman father was constantly in the society of his son, but the modern boy sees little of his parent. Instead of the son getting away from the father, in too many instances it is a case of the father getting away from the son. This is the real cause of the misunderstanding and discontentment among adolescents. They have lost the confidence and companionship of those to whom they would naturally appeal and in consequence make other social contacts far less worthy. The four hundred thousand runaway boys in America are a mute testimony to as many fathers who have previously "run away" from their sons.

A wise father will not only be subject to the call of his son but will provide for his assuming some part and responsibility in the government and operation of the home. One parent who successfully carried his boys through these troublesome teens participated with them in the direction and even the carrying of a morning paper route. Nothing can perpetuate the influence of the home like a family council in which the adolescent members are invited to contribute their opinions. Participation in family government prepares for participation in civic government and trains for self-government.

b. Companionship in school.

Social contacts that are established in school are second in importance only to those at home. The standards and practices of many homes are reflected in the behavior of classmates, so to a certain extent the influences of the home will be counteracted by the representatives of more or less desirable homes.

It must not be forgotten that groups of young people will often respond to appeals to which individuals are deaf, but that they are just as likely to listen to the recognized leadership of one of their own number as to their instructor. This suggests both the possibilities and problems of all teachers of adolescents. Like the parent they can no longer coerce but must lead and inspire. As Burr says, ''Hitherto the reins have been largely in the hands of the teacher; now they must be handed over more and more to the boy himself.'' The teacher sits alongside as an adviser rather than a driver. Where he has made a special effort to keep open the channels of communication his counsel will be sought as eagerly as that of any other recognized leader. It is the business of the teacher to so conduct himself that he will command such recognition as will assure him the control of any situation. Boys can find their leaders in teachers just as well as in their companions if it is a leadership that provides companionship.

Secret societies among high school students, while tending to socialize the individual and make him loyal and self-sacrificing to his group, have attendant evils that more than counteract their good. The fact that the counsels are secret and separate from the sound judgment of parents and teachers make them a serious detriment to character, health and scholarship. Poor parents can hardly bear the additional expense that membership in these societies occasions and it has yet to be proven that individual scholarship is advanced through this association. On the other hand, loyalty to a crowded social program involving late hours has often demoralized habits of study and diminished mental application. Nor is the secret organization free from moral indictment. Boys have acquired habits of questionable nature through loyalty to the group that would not have been possible as long as the freedom of the individual was permitted to assert itself. These distracting influences cannot be overlooked by parents who believe education involves serious work and discipline.

c. Companionship in the gang.

Next to the family and the school the social unit that is apt to make the largest contribution is the one in which the leisure time or play activities have their setting. Enlarged school activities, together with the fact that work now claims the attention of such a large number, accounts for the decline of the gang. What groups remain, however, are not only more formal in organization but also more formidable in power. At no time do these bands of boys exert a greater influence upon the individual member, and good comradeship counts far more now than at any other period of life. For this reason these unnamed groups which exist without official connection should be properly recognized and respected. The fact that boys love all sorts of club organization does not prove that this impulse can be allowed free rein. Leave your garden to nature and it will be overrun with weeds. Leave the youth to nature and he reverts to the natural man or beast. These free-lance organizations so freighted with possibilities need the counsel and companionship of a mature mind and every effort should be made to associate them with school, church or Y. M. C. A., where supervision is recognized. Tactful supervision by older minds may turn the harmful influence of such an organization into channels of helpfulness.

d. Companionship in church.

An unfortunate situation exists when adolescent loyalty to home, school and gang interferes with the development of loyalty to the Sunday-school class. The reason that the church is in so many instances the weakest and not the strongest social contact is because it has so largely ignored the interests of its young people. Churches that do not provide for the social development of their youth in an Intermediate department need not expect them to take seriously the formal religious instruction it provides. A boy of fourteen cannot be placed in the same department or class with children and he is likely to chafe at any underestimation of his years and powers. A year's difference, which means so little to the adult, is marvelously magnified in the early teens. The reason that sixty-five per cent of our girls and seventy-five per cent of our boys drop out of the Sunday-school during early adolescence is undoubtedly due not only to careless classification but to inadequate provision for their social contacts. As long as the church refuses to take the leadership in providing for the social life of its young people, so long may we expect the less desirable contacts with school and gang to shape and sear these impressionable lives.

4. The principal spiritual characteristic is conversion.

While the last days of childhood present the most promising and practical period for evangelistic effort, the largest number of conversions is to be found among adolescents. Conversion literally means a transformation and in this particular period when change is the program of life, a spiritual transformation is just as much to be expected as a physical or sexual change. Conversions, whether in childhood or adolescence, are invariably supernatural phenomena, but the reaction of the youth is different from that of the child. The work of the Holy Spirit in childhood is more likely to be manifested by a religious awakening, while in later life regeneration will be evidenced by violent and critical changes. This does not infer that a conversion requiring a more or less violent wrenching away from sin possesses more inherent spiritual value, but rather that the reaction of the older convert is characterized by a more marked resistance to the work of the Holy Spirit. Adolescence is the harvest time of all that has gone before, and the faulty preparation for life only becomes dramatically evident when conversion takes place. Adolescence is the time for religious and moral decisions, not because some wholly new factor is brought to bear on the growing young men and women, but because at that period the early impressions, moral and spiritual, manifest their natural expressions. He makes a fatal mistake who regards the adolescent period as the most important of the formative years and does not begin to sow his good seed earlier. The fact that certain favorable conditions exist in adolescence for the cultivation of the spiritual life, must not be allowed to obscure from us the religious susceptibilities and possibilities of childhood. Man does not become capable of religion at any particular age. He is always capable of it. However there are certain circumstances that peculiarly associate conversion with early adolescence.

> a. *Conversions of early youth involve the personality.*

The religion of the child and the adolescent have much in common, but while the former may be regarded as natural, the latter is more distinctly personal. There are some who find a great deal of formality in a child's religion and that of an adult. Tracy says that a child's religion possesses the formality of immaturity, while that of the adult contains the formality of decadence. However that may be, the religion of the teens should be free from both these kinds of formality. Prayers are no longer "said" daily or church services attended because it is the custom. These things are now continued or discontinued because of the personal consciousness of individuality. Habits have been formed in the preceding years, but at this time the growing mind realizes vividly that these are a part of the individuality. There comes a more objective view of self. Youth seeks a motive for his actions. Ideas of God, Christ and the church are now brought up to the bar of rational judgment. They must necessarily receive intellectual sanction or there is no inner peace or conscious unity. No longer can he receive his religion second-hand.

In childhood days there was little experience in moral self-direction. He secured permission of parents or teachers to do what was not covered by some former consent. To disobey his elders was to do what was wrong. To obey them was to do what was right. But this moral dependence is outgrown after the first twelve years. Adolescents feel free to express their own opinions. They assume the responsibility for their own behavior. Authority of the elders must now give way to the freedom of individual choice. We who thus far have been instrumental in shaping his desires must now stand aside that all religious decisions may be his own.

b. Conversions reach their peak in early youth.

Spiritual decisions may be more difficult in adolescence than in childhood, but the possibilities and probabilities of conversion are far greater now than they ever will be again. This is especially true during the two most susceptible times, the one at the beginning and the other at the close of this period. In fact, statistics state that seven times as many are converted at the age of sixteen as ten years later. There can be no question that multitudes in their teens could be reached if the church were willing to concentrate its evangelistic effort at this point. Dr. George W. Bailey, than whom none has shown a greater passion for the winning of childhood to Christ, has said, "Less time and effort are necessary for the winning of twenty children to Christ than one adult, and a Christian child is worth more in the extension of the kingdom than many adults."

The tragedy of the church is that it has permitted its young people to drift away at the very time when God speaks most directly and persuasively to the life. These drifters become the religious derelicts in every community and only a small per cent of them are brought back to the life of the church through the revival. Evangelistic effort among adults is really an attempt to correct the church's blunder in not holding its young people through the strategic teen age. If one-twentieth of this effort had been expended upon these individuals before they were twenty they would have been won to a Christian life, wreckage avoided and long lives secured for Christian service. Great as may be the achievement of turning an adult sinner from his profligacy to a new life in Christ, it is not the supreme Christian achievement. Greater far is it to be the counsellor and companion of the adolescent that he may be steadied and strengthened through his stormy teens and brought to Christian manhood unsullied and unspoiled.

e. Conversion in early youth forestalls incorrigibility.

Early adolescence is the time not only for the making of converts but also for the making of criminals. More than two-thirds of all delinquent boys brought into court are from twelve to fifteen years of age. On the other hand, the first crime is seldom, if ever, committed after sixteen. A life of crime then must date its beginnings from the early teens.

While poverty and misfortune have contributed to the downfall of youth, these agencies are not primarily responsible for a criminal career. Unwillingness to submit to the discipline of home and school are the first steps that the prodigal takes. Few boys and girls are brought into court who have not first broken away from the restraints of the home or have fled from the restrictions of school. The study of a large number of cases reveals the fact that few delinquents reached the high school, while nearly half had not gone beyond the fifth grade.

Most significant of all is the almost complete absence of Sunday-school scholars from the ranks of adolescent delinquents. Supreme Court Justice Fawcett of Brooklyn declared that of the four thousand boys brought before him in twenty-one years not more than three were members of the Sunday-school when their crime was committed. County Prosecutor O'Brien of the city of Omaha, declared that of the eight thousand cases committed to him, less than three per cent had the benefit of any religious education in home, school or church. It would seem, then, that religious education might in itself wholly determine whether the adolescent is to be a Christian citizen or an incorrigible criminal, and that the Sunday-school might serve a great patriotic as well as religious end.

When religious tendencies are implanted in childhood the conversion of youth will assure the recognition and regard for the supernatural. Regeneration recognizes God in the universe and in control of our lives. Conversion, then, makes religion the great controlling motive of adolescence and prepares him to pass safely from parental authority to divine government. A God-controlled life never requires police control.

5. Training.

Enough has been said in the preceding pages to fully convince parents and teachers that the training of the early teens is most important. The home and the church alike stand condemned when youth plays the part of the prodigal and wanders into the far country. The definite, patient, intelligent care of parents and teachers should rob the "far country" of all its attractions and make the home and the church places of delight. To further this end there should be provided

a. Organized departments.

If early adolescence is the period for the making of Christians as well as criminals, it is hard to understand why the church has not made more adequate provision for the boys and girls that might be brought under its influence during the troublesome teens. Many churches that afford adequate accommodation for the elementary division of the Sunday-school and assign suitable quarters for adult classes, do not even have an Intermediate department. Not that adults are to be denied consideration in the organization of the Sunday-school, but it should be remembered that the adult scholars are the neglected adolescents of a former generation and that boyhood is the time for study and manhood for service. For this reason the early teen group should have a separate organization with a department and equipment worthy of its importance. Such an organization will not only recognize the distinctiveness the Intermediate feels as a student in the junior high school, but will provide a program of worship fitting to his years.

Neither the Intermediate nor the Senior departments can look for a large number of recruits from the families of the unchurched, but their organization will be rendering the Sunday-school a great service if they can conserve all the boys and girls that come up from the Junior department.

b.   Organized classes.

Next in importance to the organization of the department is that of the class. This provides for the natural social tendency to form in gangs or groups of which, as we already learned, it is important that the church should assume the leadership. Class organization in the Junior department is optional, but in the Intermediate department it is imperative. Richardson says, ''Every organized class should be a vigorous social entity. Loyalty to it should not have to be compromised when, between Sundays, play considerations are uppermost.'' Not only does such an organization permit the teacher to participate and direct the social and recreational life of the teen age, but it provides educational values of high order. Youth must be trained to plan things for others, to carry responsibility. The boy or girl who has served as a class officer or committee member for a few years will know how to initiate plans and carry them out. "The majority of people who have been of the greatest service in the world," says Mrs. Birney, "are those who are capable of taking responsibility."

c.   Graded lessons.*

One of the most important matters to be considered in connection with the Intermediate department is the curriculum. It is astonishing how many Sunday-schools have been content to use the same uniform lesson for these difficult classes and then wondered why the teacher was not able to hold the scholars through the troublesome teens. How much interest could we arouse among high school students if we insisted that they repeat the studies they were supposed to have learned in the grade school? We cannot hope to interest Intermediates if we offer them nothing better than the lessons previously studied in the Primary or Junior departments.

In no other period of life is it necessary to select the curriculum with as much care. The graded lessons which provide for biographical study are well adapted to this age. The pupil who enters into fellowship with the great personalities of the Bible will be fashioned and molded by their dynamic influence. "The power of great personalities to touch the child with marvelous contagion of spirit is surpassed only by the personal influence of the individuals with whom the child is immediately associated." What a book may mean to the shaping of life in later childhood, a companion means

*The suggestions here have all been embodied in the new **All Bible Graded Series** of lessons—a model curriculum for the Sunday-school, published by The Scripture Press, Inc., 741 N. LaSalle Street, Chicago.

in moulding character in early adolescence. But biographical study should not furnish the material for all of the Intermediate lessons. As this is the great age of conversion, at least one quarter should be devoted to lessons upon "What It Means to be a Christian," with an equal number of lessons upon "Preparation for Church Membership." Special instruction of this order for six months will do more than anything else to lay the foundation for evangelistic effort.

As youth has now reached that critical stage when he requires a reason for everything he learns, the study of one quarter should be devoted to Christian evidences. Lessons that would set forth the proofs of prophecy, persecution, preservation, power, unity and circulation will establish his faith in the Bible and largely counteract the opposing voices of evolution which he is now beginning to hear in the high school. Once lead the adolescent to see for himself that the Bible is far better established scientifically as a fact than the unproved hypothesis of evolution, and he will have a respect and regard for its contents.

The Intermediate curriculum should also provide one year of synthetic Bible study. Since this is the time to deal with knowledge *en masse,* a general consideration of the entire Bible will not only secure interest, but prepare the way for a special study in later youth of such neglected portions as the poetical and prophetical books. An outline study of the sixty-six books in a one year course is now being provided in the Lutheran Graded Lessons for the Senior Department, but it would be more fitting for the last year of the Intermediate department.

    d.   Trained leadership.

The teaching of a class in the early teens is a great

task for any person. Professor Brown says, "It belongs under the head of 'big business' and will tax anyone's resources. They have a life of their own different from that of any other age group, and he who trains them in religion must know the rules of their life and must play the game accordingly." Many a successful Junior teacher has failed to hold on to her class when it passed into the teens simply because she was ignorant of the great changes that had taken place in the lives of those girls. Trained leadership that possesses sympathy and understanding with youth is most essential. Success in dealing with these young lives will depend largely upon adherence to the following laws of adolescence:

(1) Keep open the channels of communication.

"How can I gain my daughter's confidence?" asked an anxious mother of the teen age.

"Never lose it," was the wise reply.

Youth will make a confidant of some one, and happy is the parent or teacher who has always been approachable and appreciative of youth's confidences. The home should redouble its affectionate manifestations. The welcome that awaits the child when he comes into the world should await him every time he comes home. Encourage the adolescent to talk freely and never fail to give an attentive, sympathetic ear to whatever confidences you are entrusted. As the suppression of questions in childhood may destroy a personality, so the discouragement or betrayal of confidences in adolescence may destroy a soul. Hours of confidential conversation with the representatives of this age will pay years of dividends in later life.

(2) Multiply the interests.

Narrowness of interests is the great obstacle to intellectual development and the preservation of moral integrity. No real progress can be made until the mental horizon has been widened. Immoral temptations, also, can best be met by a full program of wide and varied interests. The desire to go to work, which possesses youth like a contagious fever, may be counteracted by new studies or new responsibilities which provide a limited number of hours of labor with financial remuneration. The cultivation of church contacts by preoccupying his leisure time will tend to safeguard youth in the later teens from a program of frivolity and immorality. There is almost no subject in which it is impossible to interest an adolescent keenly, and the things with which he now busies himself will continue to occupy his attention when social and materialistic temptations make their greatest appeal. To be doing something is the passion of youth, and now as never before is there a need for a careful direction of the expenditure of his energy. The success of the old plan of apprenticing adolescents lay in its provision for a supervised program of practical activity. "Every youth," says Richardson, "should do what he wishes part of the time, but should be definitely directed part of the time and should have something besides himself to occupy his attention."

(3) Command by counsel.

It is the paradox of youth that while he is stubborn he is also susceptible and that he can be guided when he cannot be governed, and directed when he cannot be driven. He will resent a direct command or a wish, but is very sensitive to suggestion. The skillful teacher, however, will avoid direct suggestion and reach the adolescent by permitting him to fulfill her wish in another way. For instance, I notice my two boys, aged twelve and sixteen, are eating their dinner with both elbows upon the table. I turn to the younger, and say, "Take your elbows from the table, no gentleman would do that." Down come the elbows and out of the corner of my eye I notice that the older boy has taken the hint and removed his elbows likewise. You would not say to the adolescent, "Henry, close the door." Henry may do so, but not willingly. He would move with more alacrity if you said, "Henry, don't you think it is rather cold in this room?" The counsel of deeds will be found even more potent than words. "Don't talk," says Weigle, "be and do. Go about your business, live straight and get things accomplished, and your influence will do what your advice never could."

(4) Control by companionship.

Youth will be controlled by those with whom they are most largely associated. A Sunday-school teacher who is willing to be an intimate companion of any member of his adolescent class is often likely to have more influence over him than anyone else. The reason why ten evangelists have designated the Sunday-school teacher as the key to evangelism is because he can come closer to the life during the years of religious awakening than either parent or pastor. A teacher, then, who is willing to be a chum may so win the confidence of his adolescent scholar as to successfully lead him to surrender his life to the control and companionship of Christ.

---

1. What is the second birth of adolescence?
2. To stress the transition of adolescence, contrast in a word the physical, mental, social and religious state of child and adult life.

3. Trace several characteristics of childhood through adolescence to adulthood.
4. What are the signs of adolescent life?
5. What are the periods of adolescence?
6. Why are adolescents likely to be misunderstood?
7. What are the four changes that mark early adolescence?
8. When are girls taller and heavier than boys?
9. Criticize the ideals of this period.
10. What is the great tragedy of early youth?
11. Describe characteristic eccentricities and suggest the best method of dealing with them.
12. Why should adolescent criticism be encouraged rather than reproved?
13. Make three suggestions regarding the mental development.
14. Why should the interests be multiplied at this time?
15. Suggest in what way intellectual capacities may be lost.
16. Why is it important to give attention to the social contacts of youth?
17. In what four places does he find his companions?
18. How may the social contacts of the home be magnified?
19. How may the teacher attain to the recognized leadership of a social group?
20. Criticize the social contacts of the church.
21. What is the difference between conversion in childhood and adolescence?
22. Make three observations regarding the conversions of early youth.
23. What is the tragedy of the church regarding adolescence?
24. How is the Sunday-school a preventative of crime?
25. Suggest four important matters to be considered in training adolescents.
26. Show the importance of the Intermediate department as a distinct organization.
27. State the objections to the use of the uniform lesson in this department.
28. Make several suggestions for a model curriculum for Intermediates.
29. Name four requisites for successful leadership.
30. Why should the interests be multiplied?
31. Suggest how commands can be given by indirect suggestion.
32. Why is it essential for the teacher to be an intimate companion of youth?

Later Adolescence

"Remember now thy Creator in the days of thy youth."—Ecclesiastes 12:1.

XIV

LATER ADOLESCENCE

THERE are no rules by which we may mark the passage from early to later adolescence. Where middle adolescence is not reckoned as a distinct division the last period of youth is generally regarded as beginning with the seventeenth birthday and extending to the twenty-fifth. While some would maintain that adult life should begin when the age of legal majority has been reached, rarely has youth fully matured mentally, socially and spiritually until the age of twenty-five. It is always unfortunate when external influences rob young people of their complete adolescence, as they require mature judgment for the selection and settlement of their life work. The Bible would substantiate our belief in prolonging the period of preparation as much as possible. God so directed that Joseph did not enter upon his life work until he was thirty. The schooling of Moses occupied forty years but even then God did not permit him to assume his great task until he was eighty. While David was anointed king of Israel at an early age, God did not allow him to come to the throne until after years of training and testing. Our Lord himself waited until the thirtieth year before entering upon his comparatively brief ministry. There are reasons to believe that the divine plan was for a twelve-year period of adolescence to correspond to the twelve-year period of childhood. The young man is far from being prepared for the fullness of adult life, so that we will find it important not only to make a careful study of later adolescence, but also to prolong this period as late as possible.

The transition between early and later adolescence is unobservable, but the characteristics are distinctive. In the later teens there is, according to Mudge, a greater interest in business matters, machinery, literature and arts, politics and social functions. At the same time the young man gives less attention than formerly to pets, collections, adventure stories and active games. As a youth he was careless, but as a young man he becomes fastidious. While the first part of adolescence was marked by collections, the last part is designated by selections. Expansion now gives way to concentration and change to control. There is more willingness to accept authority, a larger feeling of responsibility, and a greater ease in concentration. Weigle says, "Early adolescence was a time of expansion. It presented a wealth of possibilities. Later adolescence begins to select from among life's possibilities and to concentrate its energies. Life begins to narrow, but to deepen. The time of mere vision is over. Choice must be made. And with that choice comes individuality. Lives diverge."

1. The principal physical characteristic is achievement.

When the young man enters into this period he has secured at least nine-tenths of his growth and weight. By the eighteenth or nineteenth year young women have generally attained to their full stature, but the young men continue to grow, though at a greatly diminished rate for two or three years longer. The eighteenth year marks a greater retardation in bodily expansion, and the energy formerly utilized for growth can now be consumed in the development of strength and agility. The further development of the mind also contributes to a wiser and worthier use of the muscles. These physical and mental conditions, coupled with a full realization of personal responsibility, urge youth to achieve something for himself. If he is strong in body and agile in movement he may aspire to some physical achievements. This is the age when athletes develop and the training of the games of earlier years now set apart the individual runner, jumper or vaulter. Many of the records in athletics have been made by the young men of this period. In fact, men of physical achievement are generally at their best during the twenties. The baseball and football player is a veteran at thirty and the adult athlete is less likely to possess the endurance of the last years of adolescence.

Aspirations to some achievement are not limited to the athletic field. Those who have frequented the movie and worshiped at the shrine of some great actor now become possessed with a strong ambition to become a "star" themselves. Others, stirred by stories of adventure, are quite likely to emulate the heroes of fiction and set out from home as "soldiers of fortune." The aspirations of this period are characterized as much by their height as by their ideals. The mind pictures to itself the individual occupying some position of great responsibility which can be attained only after long years of service and success. Years count for little in these flights of adolescent aspiration. Plodding and preparation are forgotten in the desire to immediately realize the ambition of the moment.

If the young man has left school it is not unlikely that he will want to achieve something in the business world. The competition he enjoyed in games he now carries with him into actual life, and in his struggles to secure a coveted position he is likely to exert more physical force and effort than at any other time in life. Failure to achieve, or attain the goal, as is so often the case, will not be from any lack of energy or effort but from want of experience and seasoned judgment.

Strange to say, just at the time when the energy and power of resistance are greatest, youth is most amenable to disease. While the most favored years for life are from ten to fourteen, the number of deaths that occur between twenty and twenty-four is not exceeded until after sixty. In the recent epidemic of influenza it was found that the young men were more susceptible to the disease than anyone else. The explanation of this discovery of weakness in the midst of apparent strength is not clear. It may be due to a physical reaction from the previous period of growth or to an overdrawing of energy through excessive activity. It is apparent, however, that Providence has made a wise provision for the preservation of life during the unhealthy, unstable years and has also placed a penalty for any reckless dissipation of energy when the powers of man are at their best.

2. The principal mental characteristic is power.

Childhood is the period of the dominance of sense. Adolescence is the period of the dominance of mind. But not until the last years does the intellect come into its rightful rule. Even in early adolescence the senses are so keen and the emotions so strong as to be reckoned as an important controlling factor of the individual, but now at length the reasoning faculties attain supremacy. While the intellect in the fullness of life must always be associated with the emotions and the will, it is only in the later teens when the reason is sufficiently matured to assume control, that the individual enters into new realms of power. "The essential thing about the mature mind as distinguished from the immature mind," says Tracy, "is the power to grasp ideas in their relations to each other in a totality or system." The growth of the cognitive faculty, or the progress of the mind on its intellectual side might be most briefly described as progress in the discernment of the relevant from that which is irrelevant. In a word, judgment is the one essential requirement in all intellectual progress and development.

The criticism of early adolescence has given judgment to the thoughts and decisions of later youth. Judgment now asserts itself with a firmness that invites no alteration, and being in command of a physique that has almost attained perfect proportions, promises great possibilities in life. Where the development of the mind has not been neglected in earlier years youth now receives his birthright of power. One cannot say that the large company of boys and girls who leave school to become wage earners can no longer be included among those who are acquiring knowledge. Knowledge can be obtained from business experiences sometimes even more rapidly than from books, and a young man who is thrown upon his own resources can sometimes acquire information more thoroughly as an independent investigator than one who is under the direction of a teacher. Much will depend upon the application of the individual to his task and, above all, the way in which he spends his leisure time. School attendance requires that much of the leisure time be devoted to study, while the worker is less likely to spend these valuable hours in self-improvement. During school life the parents are generally responsible for the support of youth and feel free to exercise a considerable degree of control over leisure time, but when adolescents become wage earners and contribute to their own support, they are apt to resent parental authority in this matter. For this reason the mental growth is imperiled if not retarded when youth substitutes the workshop for the schoolroom. Self-made men are the exception rather than the rule and all who have attained to the pinnacle positions have not wasted their leisure moments. Truly

> "The heights by great men reached and kept,
>   Were not attained by sudden flight,
> But they, while their companion slept,
>   Were toiling upward in the night."

Some of the world's greatest intellects were famous in their youth. Napoleon was an army officer at fifteen and won renown at Toulon when only twenty-one. George Benthom was a skilled botanist at sixteen, and Michael Faraday was making important discoveries in physics at twenty-one. Both Byron and Bryant were writing some of their greatest poems at seventeen. Mrs. G. R. Alden published her first book at twenty, and Mary V. Terhune was recognized as an author when she was twenty-one. Michael Angelo was already a famous painter at sixteen, while all London flocked to hear "Charlie" Spurgeon when he was still in his teens. Galileo, Weber, Beethoven and Blackstone did some of their best work before they were twenty. Mental alertness coupled with physical energy has provided youth with a capacity for large accomplishments.

As there are innumerable young men and women who never begin to realize the possibilities that this period presents, it is evident that a fullness of intellectual power is dependent upon certain attainments:

a. Knowledge.

The failures of youth are not due so much to lack of conviction as to lack of knowledge. Its cocksureness, alas! often brings conclusions with a speed and complacency that is impossible where there is knowledge. The acquisition of knowledge is of the greatest consequence to the individual. It determines to a large extent the position that he will ultimately hold in life. Of the 15,433 American celebrities in Prof. John K. Leonard's book, *Who's Who in America,* all but thirty per cent are college men. Only one of one hundred of our Americans are college graduates, yet one-half of our congressmen, twenty out of twenty-nine Presidents, nine-tenths of the writers, and one-half of our millionaires are college trained. Even in the commercial world the educated man is at a distinct advantage. The statistics of the United States Bureau of Education for one of our large cities revealed the fact that pupils remaining in the high school were able to double their earning capacity within seven years after graduation.

b. Control.

The intoxication of delight from the exercise of his new powers may lead these to gallop away with the man. The forces of passion have not diminished. In all probability they have increased, but if education has proceeded along rational lines then these forces should now be subject to the authority of the intellect. Once realizing that he is worth something and can do something, he begins to more wisely conserve his time and utilize his strength. He discovers that he cannot control others until he is able to control himself and that "knowledge is power" only in so far as it is under control.

Acquisition of knowledge in itself does not guarantee

success. Charles M. Schwab, the great master of industry, in his practical and profitable book, *Succeeding with What You Have*, says, "The college man who thinks that his greater learning gives him the privilege of working less hard than the man without such an education, is going to wake up in disaster. Real success is won only by hard, honest toil. Unless a man gets accustomed to industry in school he is going to have a hard time getting accustomed to it outside. Success is built upon right habits."

Young men and women should not enter college in quest of knowledge. Education is not the quest, but the conquest of knowledge. A college is not intended to impart knowledge, but power. Knowledge is power only when it is conquered, harnessed and set to work. Moreover, education is not merely the conquest of knowledge. Its reality and finality is the conquest of ourselves. "It is not education," says Babson, the statistician, "but industry that is the mother of invention. The cotton gin, the sewing machine, the printing press, the steam engine, the electric motor are not triumphs of knowledge but triumphs of struggle, sacrifice and burning of midnight oil. Industry is not acquired in the conquest of knowledge but in the conquest of self." Until a young man's training has brought about the all important conquest of body and mind, his education is a failure. Knowledge, then, will not serve us until it has been conquered—until we have conquered ourselves.

Youth must pass through this trying transition period between parental authority and self-control, but in so far as he has acquired disciplinary habits of work and study he may assume the responsibility of self-management without danger. Self-control is not difficult where self-denial has been practiced. And in the furthering of self-denial it can be seen how religion becomes an important factor in the control of adolescence.

c. Independence.

Freedom of thought and action must accompany knowledge and control if intellectual power is to follow. At no time are children to be treated collectively, for individuality is always to be respected, but now, of all times, the individual interests are supreme. To the differences in heredity and environment must now be added the variety of pursuits that separates the young men and women into walks of life. The adolescent may have had a mind of his own throughout the years of childhood, but common interests prevented his making a declaration of independence. Now, however, he is striking out for himself and he desires the largest liberty of thought and action. Haslett says, "Few things can be of greater peril to the young man or young woman who is passing through this stage of reception and revelation and of deeper self-realization than to be spurned, slighted, passed by as one of little consequence, as one who is yet in a transitional stage and whose judgment is not to be trusted. Many youths have been discouraged and dissuaded from attempting great things in life because their ambitions have been despised."

Uniform studies and uniform tasks may be pursued until this time, but now individual variation will suggest the selection of interests that appeal most strongly. Success in any field is impossible if it does not command the heart as well as the hand and head, and distinct individualities will select distinct fields of occupation. Individuals should never be compelled to move in a circle of certain dimension. Membership in any organization that seeks uniformity of work and wages is destructive to independent thought and action. "Youth," says Dr. Brown, "needs a teacher who sees a big world to conquer, who can thrill with one who wants to go into business, to practice law, to preach, to write, to make a home, to do anything that is worthy."

This is the most fruitful period of life. The broadened outlook upon life with that intensified dynamic in feeling and will, marks this period off from all that has preceded and constitutes the preparation for all that is to follow. The long plasticity of childhood has now come to its last stage. Soon the wax will harden and no more lasting impressions can be made. The closing period of formative life should receive the most careful consideration.

3. The principal social characteristic is friendship.

The gang diminishes in size and influence as adolescents mature. Multiplied interests and diversified occupations tend to break up the gang and substitute a smaller but more select group of companions. In later adolescence we find a strong attachment for particular friends. While chums are at first selected from the same sex, sooner or later a member of the opposite sex will make its appeal. Owing to the instinct to conceal all feelings connected with sex it is not always easy to discover how much the adolescent is being influenced by someone of the opposite sex. In the early teens the boy is quite likely to be attracted to an older person who represents his ideals of womanhood. In the later teens he is more likely to select a young lady of his own age for his particular friend. It is the time for the development of chums and when this intimacy exists between young men it often ripens into a business partnership. When this particular friend is a member of the opposite sex it is not unlikely to develop into a life partnership. The later adolescent period is a time for

a. The breaking of home ties.

The attachments that are formed during these years have a tendency to make youth oblivious to any other object. The fascination of some particular friend or the absorption of a first love may lead him to utterly disregard the home folks. Others become possessed with the wanderlust, like fledglings eager to try their wings. The fact that many go away to school or give to their employment the interest and attention formerly given to the home, has a tendency to weaken the old ties. The break is most complete when the young man goes to a new community to accept a position among strangers. Opportunities to visit the home relations are apt to be few, so that the closer contacts of new friendships soon supersede the old. This transition from home environment, according to Burr, is almost as critical as the sex transition from boyhood to manhood. It is at this time that the church and such organizations as the Y. M. C. A. and Y. W. C. A. can be of invaluable help in the formation of new associations and friendships. Instead, however, of leaving the young man to be hunted up in his new environment, the home and the church, by previous communication with these Christian agencies, can safeguard youth in his hour of temptation and loneliness. Many a young man has been lost to the church because his pastor or parent has not realized the importance of having him approached by Christian associations at the hour he most needed such friendships. As a young man the author for the first time in life left home to represent a large business house in a distant city. He found himself among complete strangers, alone and lonely in a very wilderness of souls. In his little bedroom nostalgia seized upon him. He must have friends. Those about him in the hotel were of a frivolous kind quite different from the company of Christians at home. But it was just here that the church found him. The Young Men's Bible Class welcomed him and the Christian Endeavor Society showed him every attention. He was rooted and grounded in a social environment that guarded him against the temptations of his new freedom in a strange city.

b. Awakening of altruism and patriotism.

Altruism has been manifested in earlier life especially after the selfish interest of childhood days has passed away, but now it is more practical. The capacity for self-sacrifice and sustained loyalty was evidenced by our young people in the recent war. No sacrifice was considered too hard by that magnificent body of young men that so quickly responded to the call of their country. The American Legion today, numbering thousands of these manly war veterans, continues to manifest a spirit of patriotism that is not excelled by any other organization. Who would not say that this call of country in time of need has not been productive of some of the finest qualities in American manhood? The willingness of youth to sacrifice for home and country suggests some possibilities of the church enlisting his sympathy and co-operation in its world-wide program of conquest. The great trouble with so many church connections of young men is that they do not entail any real service. They fail to provide a program that will awaken the heroic qualities of manhood. As well might a volunteer be inspired to enlist in an army in the time of peace.

Unless the church sounds the militant note and provides a program that will call for individual sacrifice and service, it is not likely to make its appeal to the young people in its midst. "Give the youth responsibility," says Weigle, "make him feel that he is a worker along with you toward the same ends, instead of being himself the object of your endeavor. You need not work to make a man of him. He will make a man of himself."

Altruism of later adolescence depends largely on the development of group loyalty in early adolescence. Where this social spirit is lacking a man can be neither wholly civilized nor Christianized. "Loyalty to the small group," says Burr, "is the foundation upon which may be built, step by step, a higher and higher loyalty; first loyalty to gang, then to class, then to school, city, country, humanity and God."

c. *Manifestation of mating and homing instincts.*

In the early teens all the interest that was manifest in the opposite sex was largely superficial. There was little serious thought given to such matters as marriage and home. But at this more advanced age the realities of life more firmly grasp the individual and he no longer thinks or speaks so lightly of this personal relationship.

These more serious attachments of the teen age are not all detrimental. Many a young man has been kept from moral evil by the friendship of a pure girl who unconsciously exerted a greater influence upon him than parents and teachers. There is a danger, however, that the obligations of home life will be assumed before the young people are fully prepared and equipped for its responsibilities. Maturity of judgment, if nothing more, is required for the selection of a life partner and seldom does the adolescent mature intellectually until he has entered the twenties. The decisions that young people make in the teens are quite likely to be reversed by the better judgment of the twenties. For this reason youth should be helped by parents and teachers to realize that he is not yet a finished product. The main business that ever needs to be set before our young people is that they are getting the physical, mental and moral training which will enable them to do an adult's work. "Youth must be made to feel that before he can become a lover he must become a man." This preoccupation in the main business of preparing for life is undoubtedly the best preventative for the evils of premature love making.

A wise Sunday-school teacher, whom it was the good fortune of the writer to possess during this period, made a point never to ridicule or reprove him for his youthful attachments. On the other hand, he constantly held before him the importance of finishing his college course and gaining a degree before settling down in life. As a result, by the time the college and seminary work had been completed there was present that maturity of judgment and fuller understanding of life that made possible a wise choice.

4. The principal spiritual characteristic is instability.

These are the years when religious interest fluctuates. The new freedom into which youth enters when he severs the old ties of church and home is bound to manifest itself in his relation to spiritual things. Only the strongest habits established in earlier life can prevent the youth from at least being shaken by the temptations that now confront him. Many young men have seasons of actual irreligious feelings and tendencies. With some these seasons of doubt and disinterest are of brief duration but in others they are prolonged and difficult to overcome. The return to faith on the other hand is often accompanied by unusual religious activity. He is willing to undertake a church program of progress that his elders will assume with reluctance. Indeed, all pastors know the potential possibilities for an advanced movement that lie in the enthusiasm and energy of their young people. It is to their commanding interest and consuming zeal that they frequently appeal when adults shrink from the magnitude of the undertaking. The unsteadiness of spiritual interest and conviction is intensified by

a. *Certain hindrances.*

In the latter teens and early twenties most young people pass through a period of

(1) *Doubt.*

The student in college who has learned to reason out the facts of science finds difficulty in accepting on faith the truths of Scripture. Where no provision has been made to ground youth in the infallible evidences of the Bible, he will be sure to question the basis of its authority. The working boy is apt to be influenced by the popular writers in newspapers and magazines whose conceptions of science are often superficial and imaginary. Agnostic, prejudiced writers seeking to please a popular fancy, may prove dangerous leaders of youth in sowing seeds of doubt and negation. But aside from these external influences young people are moved to doubt from within. Reason has come to the throne and lacks the experiences of later life. They refuse to believe what they cannot understand. "He can no longer be content with the old answer that some things are mysteries," says Weigle. "Youth acknowledges no mysteries. He turns to doubt."

Commonly these doubts have been considered a sin. Youth is upbraided because of his lack of faith. But unbelief is common to man. Imperfect instruction and training cannot provide perfection, and doubts will of necessity arise to reveal defects in the nurture of earlier years. It is better not to chide or criticize adolescent doubts. Rather he should be the subject of our prayers and the object of our sympathy. We need to heed the apostolic injunction: "Brethren, if a man be overtaken in a fault, ye which are spiritual, restore such an one in the spirit of meekness; considering thyself lest thou also be tempted." A wise teacher will not argue nor antagonize. Rather he will say, "I can understand how you find difficulties in the Bible. While all these things are clear to me now in the light of greater knowledge and experience, there was once a doubting time in my life." Generally doubt does its work and vanishes. Constructive criticism gives way to conviction. Youth must be commended rather than corrected for seeking to "prove all things." With the sympathetic counsel of one who has passed through like experiences and has arrived at strong convictions, youth may be depended upon to "hold fast that which is good."

(2) Worldliness.

As youth grows into adult life he is quite likely to experience a spiritual poverty that so widely prevails as to be almost general. In the buoyancy of good health and high spirits life offers much in pleasure and profit, while death seems a long way off. Material things loom large upon his horizon and spiritual needs are little appreciated. In the vigor of manhood he is eager to enter the struggle for fame and fortune. "He rejoices like a strong man to run a race" and has every confidence of ultimate success. Lack of experience blinds his vision to the wrecks of time of which the wisdom of years has knowledge. A greedy world tempts him by offers of vast material gain, and where there is no moral force, no spiritual vision, that appeal will be all-powerful. Experience would tell him that a "man's life consisteth not in the abundance of things which he possesseth" and the wise counsel of his elders would suggest that the making of a life was of infinitely more importance than the making of a fortune. But alas! Youth is inclined to close his eyes to the failures of his predecessors and turn away from the advice of those who have walked the pathway of life. "Youth is a good companion," says Bacheller, "but a poor leader. Life with most men today is largely a process of getting rid of the wisdom of youth so as to make room for something better. The first step toward success is to overcome the conceit of one's youth."

b. Certain helps.

Home training and environment of a religious nature will tell as never before in tiding youth over this critical period. In addition to the strength of right habits and faith in divine leadership, youth will be assisted by a

(1) Deepening love of nature.

The soul of adolescence is now stirred by contact with the natural world in a way that is hard to explain. The solemn stillness of the woods, the majesty of the mountain, the power of the ocean and the wonder of the stars —all these have a fascination that is electrifying and elevating. These feelings usually go deep and move the soul. Youth is made to feel that nature understands him and believes in him. Dr. Lancaster found that 640 out of 700 whom he questioned confessed that they experienced a love of nature. This perception and appreciation of God's handiwork not only add immeasurably to the joy of living but tend to neutralize the mechanistic materialism that engrosses youth in his efforts to make a place for himself in the world. The power to perceive the beautiful is closely related to the power to recognize purity and holiness, and the admiration and awe for the perfection and power of creation leads to a greater appreciation of the Creator. Next to love of God and love of home, nature is the greatest force in human knowledge that makes for righteousness.

Statistics tell us that forty-eight per cent of the theological students are recruited from the farm. Does not this argue in favor of an environment and education that contains in its curriculum so many studies in nature? Certainly a course in natural theology is closely allied to studies in revealed theology. It was most unfortunate when our educators yielded to the demands of a materialistic age and substituted bookkeeping for astronomy in the curriculum of the high school. The business of youth is not the making of a living but the making of a life, and in the eagerness to provide "practical" studies great spiritual values have been sacrificed for materialistic gains of far less consequence.

(2) Increased vigor of will.

While the religion of the child is natural, that of the youth is personal. It is free from the formality of childhood or the immutability of adulthood. Under favorable conditions personal religion should be full of vitality. Religious practices and observances which have been taught and have grown habitual should now become instinct with life and significance. An appeal to the will power of young men and women in moral and religious matters should not be in vain. Once let them realize that the appeal is to this power which is relied upon to undertake and complete their project, and much has been done towards its accomplishment.

During the time the writer was working his way through college it was necessary upon one occasion that he raise a certain amount of money in a given time in order to complete his studies. His Sunday-school teacher had no means to assist him but as a companion and confidant gave him excellent counsel. He suggested that men of means might be solicited to make a loan in this emergency. As there was no security to offer other than the word of an ambitious student, the required sum would of necessity be made up of small amounts. Day after day the student trudged from one office to another and often without success. In his discouragement he would call up his teacher and confide his difficulties to him. After listening attentively the wise counsellor would simply say, "Are you going to give up?" Back over the telephone came the determined reply, "Never!" The teacher had appealed to the will power of the young man and that was sufficient to overcome all obstacles. When success was finally achieved he sad, "My boy, you have gained more in the experiences of the last month than you would have secured in two years at college." Such a teacher who understands young men and knows best how to help them help themselves may accomplish more for youth than anyone else.

5. Training.

The Senior or Young People's department of the

Sunday-school covers a period that is more than twice the length of any of the preceding departments. Large classes also take the place of the small groups of boys and girls which it was found expedient to limit to a maximum of eight. The reason that this longer period and larger group is now permissible is because life has become more settled and habits more fixed. Physical, intellectual, social and spiritual changes are not pronounced after the seventeenth year. The development which is still in progress is far more retarded than in earlier life. It is safe to say that the foundations of life have now been so well established that youth experiences fewer changes in the last seven years of adolescence than in any of the preceding periods. This fact suggests that we carefully reconsider Miss Lynch's all-important reflection, ''If you train your children carefully until they are seven years old, they are already three-quarters educated,'' and redouble our efforts in years when life is still in the making.

However, while young men and women change less than boys and girls they differ more among themselves. Individuality is never as marked as now. The diversity among pupils at this point constitutes a real problem to the teacher. While some in the class are pursuing their studies in high school and college, others have already assumed the responsibilities of life. In the same class we will find the lively, light-hearted student and the more sobered lad of the workshop who has already begun to walk beneath the heavy burdens of life. Certainly these distinct groups ought to be in separate classes but this is not always possible nor practical. For this reason it is highly important that the teacher be well prepared and well adapted for the work of this department. Large classes will of necessity require better teaching since it is a recognized law in pedagogy that the skill to teach twenty must be more than double the skill to teach ten. While there may be many teachers who can care for eight pupils there are comparatively few who can teach large classes well. Senior teachers, then, should be chosen with care.

The large class does not mean that individual instruction is no longer essential. Probably at no other period does the individual require as much attention. Each member needs personal guidance, encouragement and friendship. Moreover youth requires a teacher who sees a big world to conquer and who can feel the youthful interest and enthusiasm of the scholar who wants to go into business, to practice law, to alleviate suffering, to preach the gospel or do anything that is worthy of life. The absolute prerequisites for a teacher of seniors has been summed up by Dr. Brown as follows: "Knowledge of youth, attractive personality, confidence in the good qualities of youth and a determination to bring out and develop these qualities." After a wise selection of a worthy teacher has been made, training of later youth may be furthered through

a. Class organization.

The relationship between class and department organization in the Sunday-school may be likened in the American republic to the relation between the states and the nation. National supremacy invested in the government at Washington does not violate the sovereign rights and responsibilities of each state. While the states are united for organized strength and protection, each exists as a unit of government in itself. In like manner in the Sunday-school the department organization has for its purpose the protection and promotion of that fundamental triad, the teacher, the lesson and the class. At no time should its executives or its exercises overshadow the all important work of the teacher. The necessity of frequently changing the program of little people as well as providing them with instruction in worship lengthens the platform exercises and magnifies the office of superintendent in the lower departments. As the child grows older, however, the department organization gradually yields its place and power to the increasing importance of the class organization.

Thus in the senior and adult groups, while department organization serves a useful end, it is at all times subservient to the more important organization of the class. Not only do the larger classes make such units possible, but the large variety of interests represented among older people renders group interest and activity more vital than department classification. College men sometimes find more interest in a class especially arranged for their number, while a class for young mothers is more likely to make its appeal when other provision has been made for an unmarried group. Classes can be successfully built up from common contacts in life so that the widest latitude and the greatest freedom should be permitted young people and adults in the formation of independent groups.

The rise of the class organization to a place of first importance renders essential

(1) Class rooms.

In no department are separate rooms more desirable. Chairs with an arm rest for writing will appeal to the young student and a blackboard and maps are indispensable for platform work. Here for the first time the lecture method of teaching is permissible and maps and illustrations will be more needed than ever. For the best results it would probably be wise to allow a certain amount of discussion to follow the presentation of the prepared lesson.

(2) Self-government.

The success of the Young People's Society of Christian Endeavor has in no small measure been due to the officers and committee chairmen being chosen from among the young people. Not only does the interest but also the training for church responsibilities demand such procedure in the senior class. The class as well as the department should select its own officers to administer the affairs and assume the responsibility of the organization. Adults will guide rather than govern and as wise counsellors encourage the young people to provide and promote their own program. This applies to a service of worship fully as much as to a business meeting. Leaders will preside and members will participate in all proceedings. Only in the presentation of the lesson will the teacher have exclusive direction.

(3) Social contacts.

Somewhere during the period of later adolescence young men and women will form social contacts. It may be in the factory or on the farm, in the school or on the street, but happy are those people whose acquaintance is furthered in the shadow of the church. At this time when the desire for social life is the strongest the proper mingling of young people in pleasant fellowship is essential. The church that is willing to recognize and cultivate this social life is rendering a priceless service to God and country. To provide a Christian atmosphere for social contacts is to lay the foundations for Christian marriages and Christian homes with all their far reaching influence for heredity and environment. The social committee is a most important agency in the organization of a senior class and its service to church and community, although indirect, should be fully recognized and encouraged.

(4) Class activities.

Enough has been said of the desire of youth for achievement, to emphasize the importance of a program of activities if interest is to be maintained. And it is not only important that they have something to do but that the task be adequate for their age and ambition. More than one pastor has discovered in his young people the potential possibilities for undertaking extraordinary assignments. "Adequate tasks for these vigorous, restless spirits," says Burroughs, "are not easy to find, but find them we must if we are to serve the highest interests of the energetic and resourceful youths."

The organized class offers an unusual opportunity for the planning and promoting of various projects, such as providing musical talent for the church choir, conducting street meetings, organizing and operating a mission Sunday-school, opening up a reading room for working boys, providing a Thanksgiving dinner or a Christmas surprise for some neglected home, and financing innumerable missionary or charitable enterprises. Opportunities for service that can be rendered the class, the school or the church should constantly be presented. The eagerness of our young people to serve and their willingness to work is remarkable. Once the interest is aroused there is no limit to the time and energy that they are willing to expend. And that this energy may be expended in worthy achievement it is perfectly legitimate for the church to recognize the organized class as its employment bureau.

b. Appropriate curriculum.

It is unfortunate that so few Sunday-schools have given careful thought to the curriculum of the Senior department. Five out of six Sunday-schools offer nothing better than the uniform lesson and the remaining sixth in their provision of electives have not met the real needs of this period. If an oft repeated uniform lesson cannot hold the interest in the early teens, what hope may be entertained that added years of familiarity will render such lessons more pleasing to young people? Nor is the problem met by offering a course of electives. Even in the preparation of a high school curriculum it is recognized that too many electives interfere with a well balanced course of study. In like manner electives in the Sunday-school may occupy important years that should be spent in perfecting and completing the pupil's knowledge of the Bible. Most of the electives offered today are not an exploration of unstudied portions of the Bible but topical lessons based upon biblical material with which the scholar is already familiar.

It has been pointed out that the curriculum of early adolescence should be of a general scope in order to prepare and interest youth in a more specific study of the unexplored portions of Scripture. Bible proofs prepare him to find profit in the perusal of every page of God's Word, while a synthetic survey of the entire content reveals new pathways to be more fully explored later. Having now received nine years of graded instruction the senior should look forward to completing his study of the entire Bible in the three remaining years.

The first year could be most profitably spent in a study of doctrine. It is true that some doctrine must of necessity be taught before this period if the child is to accept Christ and unite with the church, but he is now better able to fully comprehend the truths that he earlier accepted in faith. Most of the material for these lessons should be taken from the epistles which until this time have been difficult to understand.

The second year should be devoted to a study of the poetical books. In thirty years of the uniform lessons not more than sixty-seven selections have been taken from the two hundred and forty-three poetical chapters of the Bible. The natural theology that abounds in Job and the Psalms is peculiarly fitting for the deepening love of nature that now characterizes the soul of adolescence. In like manner the lessons of Proverbs are of great assistance at that time of life when youth is passing through his moral and spiritual struggles. Ecclesiastes was likewise written for this very hour of worldly allurement when material things loom large upon the horizon and spiritual needs are little appreciated.

The last year should be devoted to studies in the prophetical books. In his Bible proofs with which he familiarized himself in earlier years, youth discovered that prophecy was one of the great outstanding evidences of the infallibility of God's Word, and with the knowledge thus imparted, it will not be difficult to interest him in this vast unknown and unexplored portion of Scripture.

After the Sunday-school pupil leaves the high school it is difficult to provide a common course of study for students so widely separated in various pursuits of life. Electives may be submitted for advanced work, but the most practical and profitable plan will be the provision of a teacher training class. Not only are the future needs of the Sunday-school guaranteed in this way, but young people are definitely pledged to devote their lives to a very important ministry of the church. Such a course can be arranged for the regular Sunday-school sessions and still meet all recognized standards.

c. *Vocational appeal.*

It is during the years of later adolescence that great life decisions will be made. If the burdens and responsibilities of life have not already been assumed the choice of vocation will now be made. As a companion and counsellor the teacher has abundant opportunities to steady the heart and direct the purpose towards a lofty aim. Not that any effort should be made to act for the individual. Even if a worthy work is selected youth will fail in its pursuit unless he enters upon it with enthusiasm. But the positive attitude of the teacher to all manly tasks will lend its influence toward the decision of this question on a lofty plane.

In the days that youth is walking in the valley of indecision the teacher can tactfully direct his attention to

(1) *Christian stewardship.*

To counteract the alluring opportunities for acquisition that the world offers, some one must point out the obligations that accompany possession. Young men must be cautioned that Providence has a large part in production and that personal property is far more dependent upon God and society than the efforts of the individual. Production in the last analysis rests upon the soil, sunshine and the showers, while property values are largely dependent upon the presence of a population. The contribution of the individual to production in most instances is not more than five per cent and he needs to be frequently reminded of nature's provision:

> "Back of the loaf, the snowy flour,
>   Back of the flour, the mill;
> Back of the mill the wheat and the shower,
>   The sun and the Father's will."

Again someone must point out to the unexperienced adolescent the moral and spiritual dangers that accompany accumulation and distribution of wealth. It has been truthfully said that acquisition may make the money, but distribution makes the man. What a young man earns in the daytime he may put in his pocket, but what he spends at night he will surely put into his character. Wealth that is hoarded or lavished upon self is destined to be a hindrance rather than a help in climbing the ladder of life. "They that will be rich, fall into temptations, and a snare, and into many foolish and hurtful lusts, which drown men in destruction and perdition." A recognition of the large part that both God and society contribute in the establishment of material values and a realization of the eternal spiritual values that are involved in the use and distribution of material possession, will greatly assist youth in the selection of a life work.

(2) Christian heroes.

While the world is suggesting avenues that lead to achievement, attention should be called to the great men of faith. The immortal names in God's temple of fame are not enrolled in the Bible or engraved upon the pages of church history because of political conquests or scientific discoveries. The names of these humble heroes live when all others are forgotten because they contended for a divine cause and an incorruptible crown. Where expressions have been requested, young men of this age have aspired to be a Washington, a Lincoln or an Edison, but very seldom have such men as Luther, Wesley or Moody been elected as ideals. The Apostle

Paul would probably not secure a single vote in a referendum of high school students, but this might not be the case if our young people had been impressed with what Paul under God actually accomplished. Next to Christ, Paul is "the most influential figure in human history" and in one theological library of this country there are more than two thousand volumes dealing with his life and letters.

(3) Christian ministry.

A greedy age is calling men by offers of vast material gains but men of character and of spiritual vision will be attentive to the call of God. The Christian ministry today offers the largest opportunity and the greatest reward of any calling. If the young man wants to leave an indelible, eternal mark upon the world, the ministry offers him the largest possibilities. The fields are white and ready for the harvest, and to be the successors of the disciples in this generation is honor enough.

Of course all cannot go to the foreign field and all are not fitted for the pastorate, but few, if any, consecrated young men and women dare say that they are not called to the *teaching ministry*. The thirty-six million teacherless boys and girls of America surely constitute a call to which no child of God can turn a deaf ear. The greatest benefit that the present Sunday-school can confer upon its young people is the establishment of a teacher training class and the greatest achievement that can crown the work of any teacher is the enlistment of all the members of her class in the teaching ministry. Charles W. Brewbacker says: "One cannot be active in the exercise of leading, teaching and training others without the blessing coming back upon himself. Personal growth. self-improvement. the widening

of one's usefulness in the world should in themselves
be incentive worth while and a stimulus to greater usefulness and efficiency.''

No office has been more highly magnified in Scripture than that of the teacher. God has created a countless multitude of worlds—suns upon suns, system upon
system, universe upon universe, immensity beyond all
comprehension. Yet the inspired writer in endeavoring
to magnify the reward of the Sunday-school teacher
transcends all earthly comparisons and likens the bril-
liancy and permanence of her work to the greatest
things of which the mind could conceive: ''They that
be *teachers* shall shine with the brightness of the firma-
ment; and they that turn many to righteousness as the
stars for ever and ever.''

> "A builder builded a temple,
>   He wrought it with grace and skill;
> Pillars and groins and arches,
>   All fashioned to work his will.
> Men said as they saw its beauty,
>   'It shall never know decay,
> Great is thy skill, O builder!
>   Thy fame shall endure for aye.'
>
> A teacher builded a temple
>   With loving and infinite care,
> Planning each arch with patience,
>   Laying each stone with prayer.
> None praised her unceasing efforts,
>   None knew of her wondrous plan,
> For the temple the teacher builded
>   Was unseen by the eyes of man.
>
> Gone is the builder's temple,
>   Crumbled into the dust;
> Low lies each stately pillar,
>   Food for consuming rust.
> But the temple the teacher builded
>   Will last while the ages roll,
> For that beautiful unseen temple
>   Is a child's immortal soul."

1. How does the Bible substantiate our belief in prolonging the preparatory period of adolescence?
2. Contrast early and later adolescence.
3. Suggest several aspirations of youth for achievement.
4. Discuss health conditions of the early and later teens.
5. Why is the use of leisure time an important factor in attaining mental power?
6. Name a few men who became illustrious in their teens.
7. What are the three things that give mental power to youth?
8. How does the acquisition of knowledge greatly improve adolescent opportunities?
9. What has self-control to do with success?
10. How may membership in any organization seeking uniformity of work and wage be detrimental?
11. Discuss the friendships likely to be made in the later teens.
12. What valuable aid can the church be when the home ties are broken?
13. In what way has the church failed to awaken the heroic qualities of manhood?
14. What is the best preventative for the evils of premature love-making?
15. Discuss the spiritual instability of later youth.
16. Name two hindrances and two helps in spiritual growth.
17. How should the teacher deal with prevailing doubts?
18. Suggest one reason why nearly one-half of our theological students come from the farm.
19. How may the power of will be appealed to successfully?
20. Why is a longer period and a larger group permissible in the Young People's department?
21. What conditions render teaching more difficult in this department than any other?
22. Suggest three important matters to be considered in the training of young people.
23. Discuss the purpose of department organization and its relative importance to the various age groups.
24. Why are separate rooms especially desirable for young people's classes?
25. How should a class organization be constituted?
26. Why is a program of class activities important?
27. Outline a model curriculum for this period.
28. Why is a teacher training course practical for the later years of adolescence?

29. In what way may the teacher assist youth in the selection of a vocation?

30. What is the value of emphasizing Christian stewardship at this time?

31. Why should the call of the teaching ministry be presented to every young man and woman?

32. What is the teacher's reward?

BIBLIOGRAPHY

Alexander, John L.—*Boy Training.*

Arlitt, Ada Hart—*The Child from One to Twelve.*

Athearn, Walter Scott—*The Church School. The Minister and the Teacher. Religious Education and American Democracy.*

Atkinson, William E.—*Value of the Sunday School.*

Baker, Edna Dean—*Parenthood and Child Nurture.*

Baldwin, M. J.—*The Juniors—How to Teach and Train Them.*

Beard, Frederica—*Beginner's Worker and Work.*

Birney, Mrs. Theodore W.—*Childhood.*

Blanchard, Phyllis—*The Adolescent Girl. Teen Age Tangles.*

Brown, Frank L.—*The City Sunday School. Plans for Sunday School Evangelism.*

Brumbaugh, Martin G.—*The Making of a Teacher. The Relation of the Teacher to the Curriculum. The Teacher.*

Bryant, S. C.—*How to Tell Stories to Children.*

Burr, H. M.—*Adolescent Boyhood.*

Burritt, E. G.—*The Pupil and How to Teach Him.*

Burroughs, P. E.—*The Present Day Sunday School. Building a Successful Sunday School.*

Cather, Katherine D.—*Educating by Story Telling.*

Chapman, J. Wilbur—*Spiritual Life of the Sunday School. The Personal Touch. The Personal Worker's Guide.*

Cheley, Frank H.—*Job of Being a Dad.*

Croswell, James G.—*Amusements of Worcester School Children.*

Dobbins, G. S.—*Working with the Intermediate.*

DuBois, Patterson—*The Point of Contact in Teaching.*

DuBois, Patterson—*Beckonings from Little Hands.*

Ferry, David William—*Back to the Home.*

Forbush, William Byron—*The Boy Problem in the Home. Child Study and Child Training.*

Foster, Eugene C.—*The Boy and the Church.*

Gage, Albert H.—*Evangelism of Youth.*

Harrison, Elizabeth—*A Study of Child Nature.*

Hartshorne, Hugh—*Worship in the Sunday School.*

Hayes, E. H.—*The Child in the Midst.*

Hinsdale, B. A.—*Jesus as a Teacher.*

Horne, H. H.—*Psychological Principles of Education.*

Howard, Philip E.—*Father and Son.*

Inkenberry, Charles—*Modes and Expression in Religious Education.*

James, William—*Talks to Teachers on Psychology. Principles of Psychology.*

Jeffs, H.—*The Art of Addressing Children.*

Jent, J. W.—*Primacy of Personality in Pedagogy.*

King, Irving—*The High School Age.*

Kirkpatrick, E. A.—*Fundamentals of Child Study.*

Lamoreaux, A. A.—*The Unfolding Life.*

Leavell, L. P.—*Training in Christian Service.*

Lee, Joseph E.—*New Methods in the Junior Sunday School.*

Lewis, Edward S.—*The Senior Worker and His Work.*

Lynch, Ella—*Bookless Lessons for Parent-Teachers.*

McCowan, H. S.—*The Trail a Boy Travels.*

McKinney, A. H.—*After the Primary—What?* *Bible School Pedagogy.* *The Pastor and Teacher Training.* *The Top Notch Teacher.* *Guiding Boys Over Fool's Hill.*

Martin, A. W.—*Worship in the Sunday School.*

Mudge, Leigh E.—*Psychology of Early Adolescence.*

Norlie, O. M.—*An Elementary Christian Psychology.*

Ost, A. B.—*The Bible and Our National Life.*

Painter, F. V. N.—*Luther on Education.*

Pasma, Henry K.—*Things a Nation Lives By.*

Pell, E. L.—*How Can I Lead My Pupils to Christ?*

Schmauk, Theodore E.—*How to Teach in the Sunday School.*

Sheridan, Alma—*Life in the Making.*

Squires, Walter Albion—*A Parish Plan of Religious Education.* *Psychological Foundation of Religious Education.* *Religious Educational Movements of Today.*

Stearns, Alfred E.—*The Challenge of Youth.*

Sudlow, Elizabeth W.—*All About the Primary.* *All About the Juniors.*

Thomas, Marion C.—*Primary Worker and Work.*

Thompson, D. P.—*Winning the Children for Christ.*

Thompson, James B.—*Handbook for Teachers with Young People.*

Tracy, Frederick—*The Psychology of Childhood.* *The Psychology of Adolescence.*

Trumbull, Henry Clay—*Individual Work for Individuals.*

Verkuyl, Gerrit—*Adolescent Worship.*

Wallace, Archer—*Stories of Grit.*

Weigle, Luther—*The Pupil and the Teacher.*

Whitley, Mary T.—*Study of the Little Child.* *Study of the Primary Child.* *Study of the Junior Child.*

Woolston, C. H.—*The Gospel Object Book.*

U. S. Government Publications—10 cents:

Thom, D. A.—*Child Management*, Bureau Publication No. 143. *Guiding the Adolescent*, Publication No. 225. *The Child from One to Six—His Care and Training*, Publication No. 30.

APPENDIX

I. Child Crime and Religious Training

There can be no question that the present epidemic of crime in America is due to the woeful *neglect of child training.*

Month by month the evidence piles up that a deluge of crime is engulfing America. The daily press, the magazines, and the reports of committees and organizations having to deal with these matters, all agree that crime is rapidly on the increase. A national committee composed of prominent jurists and statesmen, reporting their findings upon the prevalence of crime, made this significant statement: "Crime in the United States has reached appalling proportions, and unless checked will carry the nation on to anarchy." Murder, theft and arson and all other crimes today are from five to ten times as frequent in the United States as in any other country in the world. In New York City alone there are twelve times as many murders as in London, in fact, a greater number than in France, Italy, Germany or any other known nation. While the population in Washington, the nation's capital, has increased 32 per cent in the last ten years, murder has increased 271 per cent, manslaughter 250 per cent, murderous assault 307 per cent, and illegal liquor traffic 4500 per cent. Today the nation's capital is 2000 per cent more murderous than London, and 300 per cent more drunken than Paris. The American Bar Association recently declared that in major crimes America is now the most lawless civilized nation on the globe. Competent authorities estimate that more than ten billion dollars are stolen each year, while in the same time there are twelve thousand murders and sixteen thousand suicides. A quarter of a century ago one out of every thirteen marriages resulted in a divorce, but today every seventh marriage terminates in the court room, a notorious record that cannot be equaled by any other nation.

Most Criminals Are Children

But the most startling fact that confronts the nation as it rides upon the crest of a great crime wave, is that *the vast majority of the criminals are children.* Judge Charles W. Hoffman declared that of the ten million arrests in 1923 there were 85 per cent under twenty.

Four young men, three of them just past twenty-one years, were recently sent to the electric chair in Brooklyn for the cold-blooded murder of two bank messengers. Judge James C. Cropsey, who sentenced them, said, "The age of these criminals is not uncommon. Most of the criminals today are boys and young men. To be exact, more than 80 per cent of them are less than twenty-five years of age."

The report of the prison commissioner of the state of New York notes with horror that a large percentage of the criminals of today are mere boys and girls. "There is no doubt that the terrible situation portrayed by the prison commissioner exists," states Chief Magistrate McAdoo of New York. "My own experience shows," he adds, "that nearly all present offenders, particularly in crimes of violence, are from sixteen to twenty-five years of age." An inspection of the Tombs prison in New York City showed that it contains 122 boys between sixteen and twenty-one, many of them unconcerned about the seriousness of the situation they are in. George W. Kirchwey, of Sing Sing Penitentiary, declares that half of the inmates are under twenty-five years of age.

The major crimes of today are committed by boys who were in knee-trousers when their older brothers went forth to fight in the World War. A study of comparative ages of persons convicted of major crimes before and after the war, indicates that whereas the average age of the criminal in 1913 was twenty-nine years, in 1923 it was twenty-one years. In most states there was no special law against automobile stealing as early as 1913, but in 1923 the average automobile thief was nineteen years of age, and 85 per cent under twenty-one. In other words, more than half of the automobile thieves are boys of high-school age.

Juvenile Criminals Without Religious Instruction

There can be no question as to the cause of juvenile crime. It cannot be successfully traced to physical environment. In no other country are children so well cared for as in the United States. They are well clothed and well fed and have better surroundings than the children of any other nation. Nor is our juvenile crime due to any intellectual oversight. More than a billion dollars is annually spent in the maintenance of our magnificent public school system, and our American boys and girls have intellectual benefits that European and Asiatic children might well covet. Jurists, journalists and educators are agreed that *the prevalence of crime among children is due to the neglect of religious education.*

Judge John F. McIntyre, of the Court of General Sessions,

New York City, has given twelve reasons in order of their importance why youth goes wrong. First and foremost he places the lack of religious training in childhood, and closely following it, the absence of parental authority and discipline. He is quoted as saying, "It makes no difference what your faith may be—Buddhist, Catholic, Jewish, Protestant, Mohammedan—instill in your children in infancy the moral principles of that religion. Encourage obedience to them during childhood, and send them out into the world equipped with a definite set of religious standards. Such a boy or girl almost never finds his or her way into the criminal courts. All court officials with whom I have discussed this subject have agreed that this is the one great safeguard which can—and must—be thrown around our young people."

Judge Edward F. Waite, of the District Court of Minneapolis, speaking of the most alarming increase among young men of crimes of extreme recklessness and violence, says, "As to the causes of this I have thought not a little. I should mention two outstanding causes. First and most fundamental, is the breaking down of religious training in the home. Character can have no firm and lasting basis for the great majority of people other than religious faith. Religious faith comes rarely into any life save through early religious training."

Judge Marcus Kavanagh, of the Criminal Court of Chicago, in discussing the prevalence of crime, says, "Statistics from all over the country show that adolescent offenders come from broken homes. By that I mean not only homes where one or both of the parents are dead or in some way missing, but homes where the parents have lost control over their children. The first, but not the most important, lesson in teaching children obedience to their country's laws, is for the parents to teach them to obey the law of the mother and the law of the father. I have never seen a disobedient boy who grew into a successful man. I have never yet seen a disobedient girl who grew into a happy mother and a successful ruler of her own house. But the greatest and most vital lesson of all is to make the children know and feel the reign of God and their nearness to Him. The fathers fail mostly in their part here. Men leave the giving of the most important lessons to their wives. Fathers forget that children think their father the wisest of all men. His example more than anything else is their rule in after life. We would have few criminals in the country if the fathers of families would every week or so have a little heart to heart talk with their children about God and His infinite care for them."

Judge Harry G. Gram, of the Juvenile Court of Springfield,

Ohio, gives most remarkable testimony upon this matter: "I want to say in the beginning that I am not one of those who believe that the youth of today are generally headed for destruction, but the situation is certainly one to challenge parents and the public generally with its seriousness. Among the children who are brought into court for various offenses I find one outstanding and almost invariable lack. These children have had practically no religious and moral training, and often I discover their parents are indifferent to such influence in their lives and environment."

Supreme Court Justice Faucett of Brooklyn declares that out of the four thousand boys brought before him in twenty-one years not more than three were members of a Sunday-school at the time they committed their crime.

Attorney D. E. O'Brien states that during the years that he has been prosecuting for the city of Omaha he has docketed more than eight thousand cases and discovered that less than three per cent of the criminals had the benefits of any religious education either in the school or in the home.

William G. Shephard, journalist and author, who has secured international attention to this subject through his magazine articles, declares that the reason our present-day children are pitifully weak under the stress of temptation is that religion and morals have dropped out along the road in our educational process.

Woeful Neglect of Religious Instruction

The opinion of judges, jurists and writers as to the causes of child crime is well corroborated by any casual examination of the moral and religious knowledge of American children. In every instance *the tests reveal the lamentable ignorance of the Bible* that prevails among American children and adolescents.

Recent examinations of high school students in the state of Pennsylvania indicated that the boys and girls were familiar with all the prominent works of literature except the Bible. Quite an extensive survey was made during the last year in two hundred high schools of Virginia. Twenty simple Bible questions were submitted to 18,434 students. Only 46 per cent of the answers were correct. Ninety-one per cent of the boys and girls were unable to name three Old Testament prophets, 80 per cent could not name the first king of the Hebrew nation, while 69 per cent did not know how many books there were in the Bible.

Dr. William J. Cox, rector of St. Andrews Protestant Episcopal Church, Philadelphia, who has made a special study of the relation between crime and the ethical instruction given in the public schools of various American cities, is quoted as saying, "Out of 55,000 persons below the age of sixteen who have passed through the hands of the police, fewer than one-sixth have ever heard of the Ten Commandments. A New York high school that submitted a test upon the knowledge of the Ten Commandments, discovered that out of 1985 pupils only 434 were able to write anything at all."

II. The Week Day Church School.

The complete breakdown of the American home as a field of religious training and the inadequacy of the Sunday-school to meet the needs of the day, has centered attention in recent years upon the possibilities of a Week Day Church School. It will be remembered that the very successful religious instruction of the Jewish people was operated upon the intensive plan in which the home, school and church reinforced one another. The failure of modern religious education has been due to the shifting of this responsibility from one agency to another and the prevalence of an erroneous impression that each could carry on a program independent of the others. However, it is only the co-operation of these three agencies that will make possible a program that can be correlated and continuous.

The Week-Day Church School owing to the fact that it involves home, school and church, appears the most promising of any plan that has been proposed to solve the problem of providing religious instruction to the millions of boys and girls in America. The part that the home, school and church may take in a uniform program may be briefly stated.

1. *The home must assume the responsibility of the attendance of the children at all religious sessions.* There is much more that the home should do and could do, but this is the minimum of its responsibility. Sunday-schools are tremendously handicapped because the scholars attend only about half the time. When parents will be as particular to see that their children attend Sunday-school as regularly as the public school, not only will the boys and girls have a greater respect and interest in religion, but a larger amount of information as well. However, educators cannot compel school children to attend sessions for religious instruction unless the parents so request. The Supreme Court decision in the Oregon case recognized that the parent rather than the school must determine whether or not the child is to have religious training.

2. *The school must assume the responsibility of providing time and recognition for religious education.* It is questionable under the American form of government whether religious in-

struction can be legally given in the public schools, but there should be no infraction upon the policy of separation between church and state for the school to recognize whatever religious education may be provided elsewhere. In the majority of states there is no provision for or against dismissal of pupils for purposes of religious instruction. In such a case it is generally conceded that the local school authorities must decide upon their own regulations until such a time as state legislation or court decision gives a state-wide ruling. So the school can co-operate with the home and the church by allowing every child, whose parents request it, a minimum of one hour a week to attend a church school of religious education.

The influence of the school in this matter is of great importance. Not only do the pupils and parents learn that the school clearly recognizes the importance of religious training, but also that the church will be benefited by the improved teaching methods that its session will require. The contact with the school will assure the church a better attendance and punctuality on the part of the pupils, and a higher standard of efficiency on the part of the teacher than it has ever yet experienced. Still, each church will be permitted to teach religion according to its own denominational interpretation and the greatest liberty of religious thought will be permitted. Moreover, the church will keep the educational program in its own hands, and the lessons of the week will be continued and correlated in the Sunday-school.

3. *The church must assume the responsibility of providing a bigger and better program of religious education.* If the home and school are to recognize the teaching function of the church and co-operate with it, there must be new evidences of its interest and activity in this phase of the work to gain the respect of the community and to secure the co-operation of the home and the school. The church must reorganize its educational program and enlarge and magnify its teaching function. The church must bring the Sunday-school up to the public school standard of efficiency and continue its instruction in a week-day session. It means a real and definite program for all sessions, and a properly trained or trainable teaching force, and suitable housing facilities.

Such a co-operative program is already in operation in many parts of the country, and in so far as it can be extended to every locality where homes radiate around a school and a church, a successful solution of the present paramount problem will follow.